DEVELOPING SPIRITUAL
WHOLENESS

DEVELOPING SPIRITUAL WHOLENESS
Nancy Goudie

Foreword by Sheila Walsh

WORD PUBLISHING

Word (UK) Ltd
Milton Keynes, England

WORD AUSTRALIA
Kilsyth, Victoria, Australia

WORD COMMUNICATIONS LTD
Vancouver, B.C., Canada

STRUIK CHRISTIAN BOOKS (PTY) LTD
Maitland, South Africa

JOINT DISTRIBUTORS SINGAPORE –
ALBY COMMERCIAL ENTERPRISES PTE LTD
and
CAMPUS CRUSADE

CHRISTIAN MARKETING NEW ZEALAND LTD
Havelock North, New Zealand

JENSCO LTD
Hong Kong

SALVATION BOOK CENTRE
Malaysia

DEVELOPING SPIRITUAL WHOLENESS

Copyright © Nancy Goudie 1992.

Published by Word (UK) Ltd., 1992.

ISBN 0-85009-569-7   (Australia ISBN 1-86258-223-8)

Unless otherwise stated, Scripture quotations are taken from The Holy Bible, New International Version (NIV), copyright © 1973, 1978, 1984 by International Bible Society.

The quotation on page 51 is from The Living Bible, copyright © 1971 by Tyndale House Publishers, Wheaton, Illinois 60187.

Photograph of Nancy Goudie by Paul Yates. Clothes by Pineapple Studios, Covent Garden, London.

Printed and bound in Great Britain for Word (UK) Ltd. by Cox & Wyman, Ltd., Reading.

92 93 94 95 / 10 9 8 7 6 5 4 3 2 1

I want to dedicate this book to two very special people in my life—my wonderful husband and closest friend, Ray, and my son, Daniel, who has brought so much fun and laughter into our lives. I love you both so much.

ACKNOWLEDGEMENTS

I would like to thank the following people for being special in their own way:

Rhoda Baker, our secretary, who can now type in Scottish(!), after deciphering my handwriting and typing it into the computer again and again. Your practical help, Rhoda, and the happy way in which you carried it out, was and is a real blessing to me.

Sue Eamer, our administrator, who helped me with her encouraging comments, just at the right time.

Sandy Entwistle who helps when needed to look after Daniel, my son, to release me to speak or write. Thanks Sandy—all your hard work does not go unnoticed.

Noël Halsey and Clare Meikle at Word UK. Thank you for believing in me and for all the help and advice given.

All who have written letters telling me how much the programmes have helped them and all who have urged me to 'go for it'—especially the NGM teams 65dBA and Rhythmworks. Your comments and encouragements have meant such a lot!

My parents for bringing me up to know and love Jesus in

such a natural way. Thank you for teaching me, from my earliest years, to expect to hear God speak to me. I will never stop being grateful for you both.

Ray, without whose encouragements this book would never have been written. Thanks for all your creative ideas, inspiration, encouragement and help. Thank you for believing in me even when I didn't think I could do it. You're a wonderful husband and friend. I love you.

Finally my Heavenly Father, who so dramatically broke into my life at the age of six. Thank you for being my friend and for making the impossible possible.

CONTENTS

FOREWORD

Do you ever feel as if you lose God in the midst of the busyness of life? Do you ever find yourself praying to be more like Jesus and yet wondering where to begin? When tragedies come our way or temptations blow in our face, it's too late then to take a crash course in godliness. The psalmist David says in Psalm 1 that a happy man is one whose roots go deep into the river of life, for he will endure and when it is all over, he'll still be standing.

In this book, Nancy has made true spirituality understandable and accessible. She and I have been good friends for a long time and I have watched as she presses on to be more like Jesus. I have watched her in the midst of unexpected joy and uncalled-for sorrow, and I know her strength lies in her disciplined and wonderful friendship with Christ. I believe as you read through this book and follow her guidelines, you too will discover what an adventure it is to really know Jesus, to be led by the Holy Spirit and to feel the embrace of God the Father. Those of us who belong to the kingdom of God have found what every other man, woman and child on this planet are looking for. Let's not remain on the sidelines. Christianity is not a spectator sport. These spiritual health programmes will help us to jump in and find out for ourselves that Jesus is alive and well and living in the hearts of His children.

Sheila Walsh

LIST OF PROGRAMMES

* Please note these are only suggested topics. Every programme covers more than the stated subject.

Developing Spiritual Wholeness

CHAPTER 1

WHY SPIRITUAL HEALTH PROGRAMMES?

When Ray, my husband, first suggested to me that I should write a book containing my spiritual health programmes the thought seemed quite daunting! However, because of the encouraging results that I've seen in using these programmes, I felt stirred to develop the concept and offer them in book form to a wider audience.

Through my time with British Youth For Christ, Heartbeat and New Generation Ministries, God has given me the tremendous privilege of trying to help literally thousands of people who have approached me for counselling. One of the things I soon discovered in counselling was that in some cases people relied on me, rather than getting their eyes on God and seeking Him for themselves. Whilst I believe love, care and help from others is necessary, particularly in the areas of abuse, addiction etc., it can become unhealthy if dependence is put too much on people rather than on God.

When I look back over my life, I can see that in my times of greatest need, God has been my best counsellor.

I've found throughout my life that as I have cried out for help from my Heavenly Father, He has more than comforted me. He's given me advice, help, love and wisdom just when I've needed it. My parents have always taught me to expect God to speak and act today. I grew up in a home where Jesus was very real and therefore we involved Him in all we did. My own conversion at the age of six was very dramatic and left me in no doubt that Jesus is alive today.

It was years later when I was married that I needed God as a counsellor as I'd never needed Him before. Ray and I had a wonderful marriage. We were both Christians, baptised and in membership of a local Baptist church in Prestwick, Scotland. I was the chief cashier in a Building Society and Ray was involved in his family business. We had our own home and car. Life was good—or so I thought. Although I knew Ray had problems believing he was a Christian, I never knew the depth of his fears. On the outside everyone, including me, thought Ray was going on strong for God, but on the inside, along with his doubts, there were problems which caused him to live a defeated Christian life.

One day, he told me he no longer wished to live a double life. He was giving up Christianity. As you can imagine, I was devastated! He was the one I'd always looked to for the spiritual lead in our home. I couldn't believe what I was hearing. I spent the rest of the day and night in tears—crying out to God. My whole world was crumbling before me. I needed God to do something. I told God I wouldn't stop praying for Ray until He answered.

Ray went off to work the next morning and I continued to pray. I realised that unless God stepped in, my marriage eventually could be over. I continued to pray and cry out to God for Ray—but it was as though heaven was closed. The verse in Luke 22:31 flooded my mind, 'Simon, Simon, Satan has asked to sift you like wheat.' I felt I was struggling against the enemy. Satan wanted to destroy my husband. I was desperate for God to step in and do something. Around 5.00 p.m. that day, heaven opened and God spoke. If He had spoken in an audible voice, I couldn't have heard Him more clearly. He said gently, 'Nancy, stop crying. I have heard your prayers and seen your tears. I am going to do a work in Ray, and if you could see now the changes I'm going to bring to his life you just wouldn't believe it. Don't pray and ask me to do it; instead praise me for all I'm going to do.' Immediately, I stopped crying. My whole being flooded with joy. I danced around the room praising God for what He was going to do.

When Ray came home, I told him what God had said to me and what God was going to do. Immediately the same cold look I'd seen the previous day came back into his eyes as he said, 'Well, if God's said that, then He's going to have to do it—because I feel exactly the same way as I felt yesterday.' From that day on, unknown to Ray, I spent time each day praying for Ray, not asking God to act, but praising God for all He was going to do. The days and months went by—without my seeing any change in Ray. In my lowest moments, I remember crying out to God, 'When, Lord? When are you going to act?' Nothing seemed to be changing, but now, looking back, I can see that God was working behind the scenes, preparing the way ahead.

Exactly one year to the very day after God spoke to me, Ray, while in Canada, responded to a call to dedicate his whole life and future to God. God remarkably changed him and is still fulfilling all the promises He gave me concerning Ray.

What comfort and encouragement the Lord gave me to keep pressing on through a really barren year! God really strengthened me and gave me incredible wisdom as I went to Him each day to ask His advice and counsel. I am convinced that the Holy Spirit, our counsellor, is able to give us grace, love, wisdom and strength to help us through whatever situations and circumstances we face. Help from others is good and sometimes essential; however, there's nothing to beat God speaking to us direct. I'm praying that my programmes will help give you a structure whereby it will be easier to seek God and to hear Him clearly for yourself.

I know that for many, the thought of spending a longer time seeking God leaves them a bit overwhelmed and at a loss as to what to do. These programmes schedule your time and give you a step-by-step guide to help you seek God. The programmes include Bible reading, Bible study, meditation, memorising, fasting, prayer and a list of helpful questions. They are designed in such a way that they will help people who are not necessarily in difficulties, but who want to develop a closer relationship with God. The book also contains practical chapters on how to study the Bible, fast, meditate, pray and worship.

Some of the programmes are particularly helpful in areas such as rejection, child abuse, hearing from God, doubts, fears, discouragement, worship, revival and having God's heart for others. I have included programmes for one, two, three or five days with or without fasting, and also 'mini programmes' in case you are only able to give a few hours per day.

I have been using these programmes since 1989 and

the results in people's lives have been beyond my expectations. To encourage you I've included some letters from people who have already used my programmes to help them have a closer walk with God.

We are living in days where bodily exercise and good health are promoted extensively. There are many books, tapes, videos promoting good health, exercise and diet. There are diets for Hips and Thighs, Tums and Bums and exercises for muscles where I never knew I had muscles! I believe it's important to keep your body in good shape; however, I believe it's even *more* important to keep your *spiritual* health in tip-top condition.

I am convinced that living in what many believe are the last days, there is a deep and urgent need for us to have an even greater intimacy with Jesus. I am praying this book will not only help people to deal with problems, but also inspire many to have a 'healthier' lifestyle of meeting regularly with God, which will develop this 'greater intimacy' with Jesus.

I believe with all my heart that God is bringing revival to many nations of this world. God gave me a picture in 1986 of a mighty tidal wave crashing onto the shores of Britain and spreading out into many nations. God spoke and told me He was bringing a new move of His Spirit. It would be something new and fresh and we would see God move in ways we had not begun to experience. The more the years have gone by, the more I am convinced of God's preparation for a mighty move of His Spirit in this world. We need to be people who are ready, willing to work for our Lord, willing to put aside time to know Him intimately. It is important to work for Jesus, but even more important to be His friend and to know Him intimately.

I pray that my spiritual health programmes will truly be the right kind of spiritual food and the right kind of spiritual exercises to bring you into that close relationship with Jesus, that will cause revival fire to burn in your hearts and spread out into this needy world.

Do please write to me when you've concluded a programme and let me know what God has said to you and what results have come from the time you spent with Him. It would really encourage me to hear from you. Send letters to:

Nancy Goudie
PO Box 48
Malmesbury
Wiltshire
SN16 OHR

CHAPTER 2

THE PROGRAMME WORKOUT

How to Use a Programme

Before you embark on a programme, there are several preparations you need to arrange.

The Warm-Up—Preprogramme Exercises

1. You will need a notebook and pen.
2. You will need a Bible—preferably the New International Version as all my references come from the NIV translation. You may wish to have another translation of the Bible also.
3. You will need cards for your memory verses.
4. You may need a dictionary, depending on which programme you choose.
5. You may need a commentary—I would advise you to have one handy. If you don't own a copy try and borrow one from your leader or pastor.
6. You will need a clock or watch as time-keeping is very important.
7. Make sure you have a room or place you can go where

you will not be disturbed. Distractions can be a real hindrance to seeking God.

8. Select a programme which suits your needs the best. Decide how many days you can set aside to seek God. If you need help in a specific area, then refer to the list of programmes I have given on pages 13 and 14. However, any programme can be used to help you get to know God more intimately.

9. Once you have selected a programme, read through it to see if there is anything you specifically need. Decide whether to do a mini or a full programme. I would encourage you to do a full one if you can.

10. If you are doing a programme which requires you to read one of the recommended books, then make sure you have chosen a book and acquired a copy.

11. If you need a tape to help you in your praise and worship, then again make sure you have chosen one that is suitable.

12. If you are praying with your pastor, leader, counsellor or friend during the day, then make sure you have arranged for them to meet with you at the appropriate time.

13. If you are including fasting with your programme, then do prepare yourself by cutting down on tea and coffee beforehand and perhaps going on a fruit diet the day before. Make sure you have enough to drink during the day. I have given specific places where you should rest and drink; however, you can also drink at any point during the day.

14. Make sure you have read all the chapters on fasting, prayer, Bible study, meditation and praise (Chapters 3 to 7) so that you are fully prepared.

The Programme Exercises

The programmes themselves are fairly self-explanatory; however, here's some information which may help you.

1.   I have provided complete programmes for those able to give a full day or days to seeking God. However, I do recognise that for many of you, it is impossible to give that amount of time. Therefore, I have included 'mini' programmes which are taken from the complete programmes and give you four hours' work per day. Perhaps you could schedule an hour in the morning, an hour at lunch and two hours in the evening if you happen to be in full-time employment. If you are a busy housewife, then you may want to use the programme when the children are in bed. Whatever your time-scale, you can adjust the programme to suit.

2.   You will notice each programme starts at 9.00 a.m. and finishes around 6.00 p.m. but the timings I have given are not to be adhered to strictly. If it suits you to start at 8.00 a.m. or even earlier, then please feel free to do so.

    The programme is designed to be flexible, yet it is important on your side to be disciplined as well. Don't worry if you find your timing different to the timing on the programme. For example, one person may take the full hour and a half for the Bible study, whereas someone else may finish sooner—or even later. If you finish early, then move on to the next section—you never know, the next section may take you longer than I have given. If you finish later, then I'm sure you'll be able to make up the time elsewhere. The timings are only a guide.

3.   You will notice that I have scheduled several rest

periods—do make sure you rest within these times, especially if you are fasting. Try and avoid television —perhaps give yourself a rest from *Neighbours* for the day.

4. If it's impossible because of bad weather to go for a walk, then find yourself a seat at a window where you can see something of God's creation—i.e. trees, grass, sky, etc.

5. In the longer programmes I have suggested that you read a book from the recommended book list in Appendix 1. There are times within the programme for you to read the book—however, you may not be able to finish it all within the time-limit given. I would suggest you continue to read the book in the days following, or perhaps start reading the book prior to starting the programme. Whatever you decide, don't try and cram too much into the one session.

   I would suggest you read a book which would inspire and encourage you. I've included in my book list a number of books which are testimonies of people God has touched in some way. There is no problem if you want to read a book that is not on my list. My suggested list is not conclusive—so please feel free to find a Christian book to build up your faith in God. However, I would not advise you to read a heavy study book at this time.

6. Make sure you write down in your notebook everything God says to you. It's so important to keep a record of how you feel, or what you received from God at the time. Also, write out the answers to your Bible study in your notebook.

7. I often find that when I spend time alone with God something will happen to disturb me. The telephone rings or someone calls at the door. It's important to

remember discipline at this point. Obviously we need to be polite, but state quite firmly that it's inconvenient to see anyone right now and ask them to call back later. I'm sure your friends will understand.

The Wind-Down—Postprogramme Exercises

1. After completing a programme, allow time to go through all that God has said to you. Unless it's unavoidable, don't rush straight into other things. Why not fast television for the evening and allow all that God has done in you to take root?
2. I would encourage you to continue with some of the exercises within the programmes and incorporate them into your daily life, e.g. memorising, meditation, walking with God, etc. Don't forget all you have learned, but use them to get deeper into God.
3. You may want to arrange for friends to come over and pray with you once a programme is finished. Perhaps arrange a prayer group at your home or attend one elsewhere.
4. If you have been fasting remember to break your fast sensibly, especially if you have been fasting more than one day. (See page 33.)
5. I would really appreciate you writing me a letter telling me what God has done in you through your special time with Him. Do take a few minutes to drop me a line or two—it would be very encouraging for me.

Here are a few examples of the kind of letters I have received from people who have completed some of my programmes.

Sarah from London writes:

I often think, 'I must take time to study the Bible more,' but there always seem to be excuses coming up that rob me of this privilege. So, for me, taking time to fast and seek God became an ideal opportunity not only to commit a specific issue to God, but also to enjoy His presence and His Word.

I knew that I was in need of a breakthrough in a certain area of my life. For many reasons FOOD was governing my mind and way of life. On approaching you for counselling I felt quite at peace and even excited at the thought of being able to see this issue dealt with. Since, for me, it concerned food anyway, the thought of fasting scared me a little, but what really helped was having a specific programme to work through so that my time was filled and my thoughts were being renewed as I focused towards Jesus. Also, having people I could share with at the end of the day who could then pray with me was a great encouragement, since I knew I wasn't facing the task totally alone.

Through doing your programme God showed me reasons for my irregular eating patterns and other traits about my character, which I was able to surrender to Him.

He also showed me that all the pain and suffering I had undergone in the past was gone and after forgiving those who hurt me, all I needed to do was to let go and receive His healing touch. God also did two other things. He revealed how much He loves and delights in me, and I was in a place where I could receive it. Through the Bible study, He also stirred up a vision He'd already given me for my life, giving me new excitement about the plan He has for me.

Sue from Wiltshire writes:

I appreciated doing one of your programmes; not only was it great to spend so much time with God in such an organised way, but I found that through it, God really refreshed me. He gave me a new depth to my relationship with Him, emphasising His love for me and giving me a greater security in Him. I have found since, that I no longer have to rely on my feelings or experiences to tell me that God is with me—now I KNOW that this is true.

A 20-year-old girl writes (name withheld):

When I was young I was sexually assaulted by a neighbour, and then when I was 16 I was raped by my boyfriend. These experiences left me with a lot of fears, especially in the area of relationships.

When I was doing the programme, God showed me how much He loved me and cared for me. He gave me a picture of me lying on a cloud of love. This cloud protected me and just overwhelmed me and lifted me up out of my problems and fears. As the Bible says, perfect love drives out all fear.

I also had a big problem with praying in public. I could form a prayer in my head, but I just couldn't speak it out. It was as if some-

thing stopped me saying it. I was at a prayer meeting soon after I had done your programme and I was praying away, before I realised what I was doing. It was as if my tongue was suddenly loosened.

I discovered through your programmes that I can overcome my fears with God's love.

David from Lancashire says:

I found the programmes very useful in keeping my mind focused on God and what He was saying, rather than on what I was missing for dinner!

They really helped keep a structure to the day whilst leaving lots of room for God to speak. He really did use your programmes to speak into my life; not just for the present, but also giving some markers for my long-term growth too.

Thank you for taking some of the mystery out of fasting and also encouraging me to be as open with God as He is with us.

And Robin from Bristol writes:

I found your programme really helped me to know where I was with God. It helped me get closer to Him because I spent the whole day just being in His presence. I heard God speak to me very clearly and learned such a lot through the Bible study. I thoroughly enjoyed it and I really understood what was being said through the passages. Thanks a lot.

You will find more letters in Appendix 4.

CHAPTER 3

THE FASTING WORKOUT

I remember hearing of a girl who went along to a seminar entitled 'How to pray and fast'—thinking she was going to get ideas about how to pray quickly!! I'm sure she represents many who have been starved (excuse the pun) of specific teaching on the subject of fasting. The result is that a lot of people are missing out on following God's instructions and receiving the promised blessing (Matthew 6:17–18 and Isaiah 58:6). For many the thought of not eating any food for a specific length of time is horrendous. They feel the task is beyond them, so for those of you who have not fasted before let me encourage you—you will not die through fasting for a few days! The very first time I fasted—it was as though my stomach thought my throat was cut! All I could think about was FOOD FOOD FOOD! Everywhere I looked people were eating. I counted the hours away until I could have something to eat. It certainly made me realise how undisciplined I was with respect to eating.

Fasting is not easy, but I have found that if you have a goal in mind, and if you do it in a disciplined manner, then it's much easier. That's where I believe a fasting programme will help you. It gives you a structure to work through—leaving you to concentrate on the Lord and not your stomach! Others who have already worked through some of my programmes have found this particularly helpful. To encourage you, here is an example of the kind of letters I have received about fasting. You will find some more in Appendix 4.

Liz from Exeter says:

> *I just wanted to say thank you for the help I received from your programmes.*
>
> *Fasting for me has always been something that I knew as a Christian I should do—but why and how were pretty big questions that lurked at the back of my mind. Using your programmes has gone a long way to answering those questions for me. Fasting has never been very easy for me; however, I found that having my day structured was an excellent motivation for me to want to fast, and also to continue to fast for the whole day without giving up!*
>
> *The programmes are very challenging, leading me really to expect God to speak to me during the day (which He did!). The variety the programmes provide is also very important, and made me realise that fasting isn't always locking yourself in a little room with a bottle of water and a Bible! I learned how to express myself to God, and felt so happy when I knew that God was pleased with me for honouring Him by fasting.*
>
> *Thank you for the time you spent on the programmes.*

Why Fast?

There are many reasons why we should fast. I will list a few of them here for you and I hope and pray that they will inspire you.

1. To seek God and have a deeper friendship with Him.
2. To receive guidance about a decision.
3. To humble yourself.
4. To pray for others.
5. To free you from sins that have a real hold over you.
6. To seek physical, emotional or spiritual healing.
7. To ask God for wisdom.
8. To ask God to intervene in an area where you are experiencing tremendous problems.
9. To prepare yourself for warfare.
10. To ask God to anoint you for service.
11. To show God you are prepared to sacrifice in order to seek Him for what you want Him to do for you.

How to Fast

Let me answer a few basic questions about fasting:

1. What exactly does fasting mean?

Fasting primarily means consuming no food and perhaps even no water, for spiritual reasons, over a period of time. There are many examples in the Bible, e.g. Daniel fasted (Daniel 10:2–3), Elijah fasted (1 Kings 19:8), David fasted (2 Samuel 12:16), Esther fasted (Esther 4:16), Jesus fasted (Matthew 4:2).

There are 3 main types of fasting:
  a) **Partial fast**: No solid food, but liquids only or eating

simple, basic food only.
b) **Normal fast**:   No food, only water or drinks, e.g. fruit juices.
c) **Absolute fast**: No food or water.

For many the partial type of fast is the easiest, and if you've never fasted before then perhaps this is the fast you should have a go at first. Try eating only fruit and vegetables or perhaps a soup fast. When I've done a longer fast, I have sometimes eaten liquid soup only. (After it's over, you never want to see another bowl of soup again!!)

I usually stick to the normal fast—eating no food but drinking water (or sometimes drinks, e.g. fruit juice).

Some other types of fasting do not include food. For example:

A sleep fast	Getting up a couple of hours or so earlier than normal to spend quality time with God, or perhaps fasting sleep altogether and having a whole night of prayer.
A TV fast	Deciding not to watch television at all for a certain amount of time. We have often spent a week fasting television and used the time to pray and seek God. We have found this type of fast to be effective and very refreshing.

2.   How long should I fast?

I believe we should fast regularly, e.g. once a week/ month—it will certainly help you spiritually if you combine it with prayer and it will also help you physically. However, each of us needs to ask God how long we should fast and what type of fast we should do. Follow His instructions and you won't go wrong. One of the things God said to us at the beginning of Heartbeat, was that we should always fast and seek God before we went out on a mission. It was in these times of prayer, fasting and warfare that God equipped us and gave us strategy for the spiritual battle ahead. The fight for people's lives was often fought and won during these times. God really does honour the time we spend seeking Him. It is never a waste of time!

If you have never fasted before then do start slowly. Try skipping one meal first (lunch is probably easiest)— then perhaps two meals. Stop eating one morning after breakfast and don't eat again until the following morning. This would be a 24-hour fast.

If you miss breakfast, lunch and dinner, that would be a 36-hour fast. You can fast food up to 40 days—however I would *stress* that a long fast should only be undertaken if God instructs you to do so. I would also advise you to contact your doctor for advice if you are contemplating fasting more for than three days.

An absolute fast should only be undertaken when you receive direct instructions from God and should be for a maximum of three days. Do not go beyond three days as the body cannot cope without water beyond that time. It would need God's divine help for anyone to go on a longer absolute fast.

3. How should I break a fast?

Slowly! I remember the first time Ray fasted for two days —he got to the end of the fast and his appetite was enormous. He saw some cakes and sweets and gulped them all down! A few hours later, both he and his stomach wished he hadn't!! You should be very careful how you break your fast. After fasting always begin with a light meal. You should never break a fast with anything heavy— especially greasy meals. The best way is to eat fruit, vegetables or perhaps a light salad. Do remember that the longer the fast the more gradually you should break it.

During the fast you may experience headaches. These will probably be due to caffeine withdrawal. If you have been used to drinking ordinary tea or coffee, then it may be wise to cut down on these before your fast. You will certainly experience hunger pangs!—drink a couple of glasses of water to fool your stomach. Don't get discouraged if you break your fast before you meant to. Ray once took a biscuit while fasting and ate it before he realised what he had done! God will not condemn you—just determine yourself to go on seeking God anyway.

4. Should I fast whilst working?

The answer to this question really depends on the nature of your work and the length of your fast. We in NGM have often undertaken one- or two-day fasts without stopping our work. However, we would not fast during a long tour where it involves moving heavy equipment and working long hours. We would always fast beforehand. Obviously, you need to be sensible—but don't make your work an excuse for not fasting!

One word of warning. If you are on medication for a serious illness such as diabetes, heart problems, liver or kidney disease, or in fact on any kind of medication, then I would strongly suggest that you consult your doctor before going on a fast. Perhaps you could ask your doctor if a partial fast of fruit or vegetables is acceptable, or maybe try a TV fast instead.

If you would like more information on fasting then I would recommend *God's Chosen Fast*, by Arthur Wallis and *How to Fast Successfully*, by Derek Prince. Both books are very easy to read.

CHAPTER 4

THE PRAYER WORKOUT

What is prayer? Prayer is very exciting—it's certainly not boring because prayer, in short, is having a two-way conversation with God! Imagine, we are able to talk with the Creator of the universe—the Creator of all you see around you, and, even more exciting, we can hear Him talk back to us! We should communicate with Him as naturally as we would with a friend, whilst not losing sight of the fact that He is the King of Kings.

Prayer is not always easy. Perhaps you thought it was only you who finds prayer difficult, but the fact is that we all struggle at times. There are so many things to distract us. Perhaps the telephone will ring, or you'll remember something you have to do, or your thoughts will wander on to a different subject. Satan knows how effective prayer is, so he is really keen to stop you from talking to God. The most effective thing you can do is to pray. Prayer accomplishes so much. God not only listens to our prayers but acts upon them.

Have you ever felt, as I have done many times in the past, as if your prayers are hitting the ceiling and not reaching God at all? It's easy in these times to give up and yet that would be exactly what Satan would desire. There can be many reasons why this seems to happen.

1. Sin

You should ask God if there's anything you're doing or have done that displeases Him. Confess it and ask for His forgiveness. The barrier will then be lifted. Read 1 John 1:9.

2. Wrong feelings

Our feelings can be very deceptive. We must never depend or rely totally on our feelings. If we put our trust in our feelings then our faith will go up and down. One morning we can wake up 'feeling' bad and feeling as though we're not in touch with God, whereas another morning we may wake up 'feeling' good and feel we've got it all together. Never put your faith in feelings. If you do your spiritual life would be up and down like a yo-yo. Put your faith in God and His Word. What does His Word say? He will never leave you nor forsake you (Hebrews 13:5). No matter what your feelings may be—God's Word never changes.

3. God could be teaching us maturity!

Sometimes in order for us to grow, it seems as if God withdraws just a little. As He does, He allows room for our faith to grow. Will you continue to pray even although the sense of His presence is not around you? Will you trust Him anyway? This can be a hard lesson to learn—but sometimes through real pain can come real progress. Perhaps God needs you to trust Him more.

Whatever the reason—do keep on praying. God will bring His answers in time. A man well known for his prayer ministry once said the eleventh commandment was 'Thou shalt bash on.' I've made a list of some of the things that have really helped me in my prayer life.

Pray out loud

I am always amazed how many people 'think' their prayers rather than *talk* to God. You can think your prayers—but I've found that doing that leads to wandering thoughts very quickly—whereas 'talking' your prayers focuses you much more. Always talk out loud to God if you can. It will help you enormously, especially if you are not used to praying publicly.

My young years were spent in a church where women weren't allowed to speak publicly. As a result, I found it extremely difficult to pray publicly. What helped me a great deal was to talk my private prayers out loud. It not only helped in the area of concentration, but also I got used to hearing my own voice in prayer, which, believe me, is a huge barrier when it comes to praying publicly. A good number of Jesus' prayers were recorded—so He must have prayed out loud, e.g. John 17, John 12:27, John 11:41.

Be natural

You don't need to use old-fashioned language to talk to God. Talk to Him as you would to a friend. You don't need to kneel, clasp your hands and close your eyes. Do these things if you feel it necessary—but God will hear your prayer whether you are walking, sitting, lying, driving or even in a bath. I pray anywhere and everywhere! I love having a special time with God where I can kneel or sit and just have an intimate time with Him, but my friendship with Him is 24 hours a day, so therefore I chat to Him wherever I happen to be. It's so important to develop an intimacy with Him that isn't just slotted into one part of your day! It's important to remember that although He is your King and Judge, He is also your dearest and best friend!

Be specific

God loves you to be specific with Him and not just talk in generalities! I remember in 1983 when we, as a team, first reached out in faith to God for a van for the work we were doing. God spoke ever so clearly to us. He said, 'Be specific. What kind of van do you want?' So we went and checked out all the different kinds of vans—what height, depth and capacity we would need, and wrote it all down and presented it to God. We even worked out what year we would like it to be (our faith wouldn't allow us to go for a new one) and therefore what kind of price it would be. We had no money and no contacts. We were told this kind of van was very difficult to get a hold of . . . but within 48 hours of our presenting this need before the Lord, God had not only provided the full amount of money for the van, but also led us to a contact who had the exact van for sale. It was the exact year, price, measurements and was, in fact, ideal for our work. God is good! It taught us a lesson in prayer. God wants us to be specific.

Pray within your faith

Read Mark 11:22–24. It's so important for us to pray believing our prayers. There is no point praying for something if you don't believe God will do it for you. Examine your faith level. Pray within your faith limit and as your prayers are answered, you will build up more faith to see God do so much more!

Pray with others

Especially your partner—if you're married. On a human

level, it brings you so much closer to the person with whom you are praying. I just love to pray with others. On a spiritual level, Jesus promised us, 'Again I tell you that if two of you on earth agree about anything you ask for, it will be done for you by my Father in heaven. For where two or three come together in my name, there am I with them' (Matthew 18:19–20). It's good to support one another in prayer.

Pray in the Spirit

'So what shall I do? I will pray with my spirit, but I will also pray with my mind; I will sing with my spirit, but will also sing with my mind' (1 Corinthians 14:15). Paul also says, 'I thank God that I speak in tongues more than all of you' (1 Corinthians 14:18).

I find the gift of tongues essential to my prayer life. Not only does it allow me to worship and praise my Heavenly Father beyond my human words and understanding, but it also helps me in my intercession for others. There are so many times when I just don't know what to pray and I just allow the Holy Spirit to pray through me (Romans 8:26). As it says in 1 Timothy 4:14 it's important not to neglect the gifts God gives us. I believe we have sometimes demoted this gift because of controversy. I would like to encourage you to use this precious gift as I feel it is a vital part of our spiritual life.

How to Hear from God

As I said at the beginning of this chapter, prayer is a two-way conversation, not a monologue. To pray effectively we must develop a listening ear. Take time to hear God speak to you. In order to have a friendship with another person we must spend time listening as well as talking. In our friendship with God, it's so important to hear what He has to say to you. God is not dead and neither is He dumb. God is speaking today, but the problem is, too often we are not listening. There are many ways to hear God speak—allow me to list a few of them for you.

1.   An audible voice
There are many instances in the Bible of God speaking in this way. John 12:29 says God spoke and the people thought it thundered. I have never personally heard God thunder from heaven, but I do know He has spoken to some people like this in these days.

2.   The Bible
If you go away from home for some time, how do you communicate with friends? You would communicate through a letter. It's just as if God has sent us a love letter and it's called the Bible. Sometimes, when we are asking God a particular question and then we read the Bible, it's just as if a verse 'jumps' out of the page and hits us on the head. God shows us His answer through His Word. God will often speak to us in this way. Its important, however, to know Scripture as a whole and not just take a random verse as confirmation of what God is saying.

Years ago a friend of mine, who was desperate to go out with a man called John, asked God over and over to confirm if he was the right man for her. She closed her Bible and prayed, 'God, if John and I are going to get married—please show me clearly.' I hasten to add she was not even a friend of his at the time! She opened her Bible and it fell open at the book of *John*. She couldn't believe her eyes because right there on the page was the story of the marriage at Cana in Galilee. She was convinced God

40

had told her she and John would get married. Needless to say, they both married other people. We must make sure we don't use Scripture to fit what we want God to say.

3. People

God can speak to you through your pastor, leader, family or friends or even perfect strangers. A number of years ago when Ray was in Canada, he was asking God to confirm whether we should be in full-time work. He went to a church meeting where around 2,000 people were gathered to hear Brother Andrew. On his way out of the church, a middle-aged man, whom Ray had never met before, approached him and said he felt God had asked him to tell Ray a message. The stranger went on to say, 'I'm not sure this bears any relevance to your situation, but a number of years ago God called me into full-time work, but because I was involved in my family business I didn't go. Now, 40 years on, I realise I disobeyed God. If God is calling you to full-time service, then don't allow anything to hold you back.' What the man didn't know was that Ray was involved in his family business and because of Ray's love for his parents, he didn't want to let them down. What a direct word—straight from God—straight to Ray's heart.

4. A still small voice

Just as there are instances in the Bible of God speaking in a loud thundering voice, there are also instances of God speaking in a still small voice. Read 1 Kings 19:9–18, where Elijah is in a cave. He desperately needs to hear from God. First of all there is a strong wind, then an earthquake, then fire, but God was not in any of these. Then God speaks in a 'still small voice'—God's direction had come. It says in Isaiah 30:21, 'Your ears will hear a

41

voice behind you saying, "This is the way; walk in it." '
It's often like that; God comes and whispers in your ear,
'This is what I want you to do.' Some people find it
difficult to hear His 'still small voice'. Sometimes, we are
just too busy—for many it's because they haven't
cultivated a listening ear.

I found the illustration of using a radio very helpful.
When you turn on a radio you often have to pass various
voices and sounds before actually finding the station you
want . . . and even when you find the station it seems far
away and you have to fine-tune it so that you can hear the
station clearly. Hearing God's voice is sometimes like that.
There are so many voices in our heads—voices we hear
each day, our parents, friends, workmates, our own
thoughts and even the voice of the enemy, and we need to
by-pass any distractions and fine-tune ourselves into
hearing God's voice.

People often ask me, 'How do you know it's God
voice speaking to you and not just yourself or even Satan?'
All I can say is, the more time you spend with God, the
more you know His voice. Imagine yourself in a crowded
room with lots of voices and noise around, when suddenly
from somewhere in the room your mother shouts your
name. You would turn round and look in the direction the
shout came from and even although you couldn't see her,
you would know she was in the room. Why? Because you
recognise her voice—nothing would convince you
otherwise. Similarly, when you get close to God, you also
get to know His voice. As it says in John 10:27, 'My
sheep listen to my voice; I know them and they follow me.'
Again, a word of caution—we must test everything with
His written Word. God would never contradict what He has
already said in the Bible.

5. Visions and dreams

God says in Joel 2:28 that in the last days He would speak in visions and dreams. During one of our missions in Northern Ireland, I remember meeting a girl after a morning assembly in her school. She was visibly shaking. She said, 'I've never met you before and yet last night I had a dream and you were in it. I saw you up on a stage telling me, "You've got to get right with God." I came into school this morning and there you are on our school platform telling all of us, "You've got to get right with God." What is going on?' I sat down with her and explained that God was speaking to her through her dreams. It often happened that God spoke through dreams in Scripture, e.g. Genesis 37:5–11, Matthew 2:13, Matthew 1:20, Matthew 2:20. God was speaking very clearly to her.

God can also speak to you by giving you a 'mental picture' or vision. There are many illustrations of this in Scripture, not least in Daniel (Daniel 10:1). A friend of mine was trying really hard to get a picture from God during a church meeting. She closed her eyes and saw this wonderful design. She was just about to share it, when she opened her eyes and discovered it was the design of the carpet! Undeterred, she continued to seek God for visions and now she frequently gets significant pictures from God. Expect Him to speak to you through visions and dreams. Ask Him what they mean. It's so encouraging when God speaks to you in this way.

There are many other ways to hear God speak to you, but the most important thing is that we are listening! Take time to cultivate a listening ear. Don't just talk at God— listen to what He has to say. Get to know Him intimately—allow Him time and space to speak into your life.

CHAPTER 5

THE BIBLE STUDY WORKOUT

When I was younger, Bible study seemed to me to be only for vicars or ministers with theology degrees and definitely not for someone like me! Questions like How? Where? What? flooded my mind when I thought about studying the Bible. After unsuccessfully searching around for a helpful study guide, I eventually borrowed a family heirloom, and armed with what seemed the heaviest and biggest commentary in the world, I started my journey into studying the Bible. Much to my amazement, I really enjoyed the exercise and although I don't recommend you use the same Bible commentary, I would encourage you to study the Bible for yourself. It can seem a bit daunting at first, but with all the helpful study guides around today, I'm sure once you get started you'll never look back. If you haven't studied before, or find it a bit hard going to study the Bible, then I'm praying that my programmes will be the encouragement you need. They certainly gave Karen from Malmesbury the encouragement she needed:

> *My Bible study was always difficult and I could never really understand what I was*

reading. Working to the programme and spending more time with God completely changed that. It all began to have real meaning. I can relate what I am reading to what is happening in my life. I can now hear what God is saying to me; before working on the programme I never knew how to listen.

I now know that I can completely trust God in all things and He will never let me down. I knew it before, but now I believe it.

Some of the letters in Appendix 4 express similar reactions.

Although my programmes are not designed to give you a theology degree, I am hoping that they will give you a greater hunger for God and His Word. If you feel like doing further study, I've listed a number of helpful books in Appendix 1 that will enable you to do so. To help you to use the Bible studies in the programmes, I've included one here that I've already completed.

1 Timothy 1

Read the chapter three times.
1. Who wrote 1 Timothy?
2. When was it written?
3. Where was it written?
4. To whom was it written?
5. Why was it written?
6. What are the main points Paul is trying to convey in this chapter?
7. Read verse 3. What was the task that Paul had given Timothy to do?
8. The people Paul is talking about in verses 3 to 7 are

confidently affirming wrong teaching. How can we be sure we are following correct, biblical teaching?

9. Write down the things we as Christians should pursue (see chapter 6, verse 11).

10. Read verses 11 and 12. What is Paul's commission from God and when in Scripture did He appoint him to His service?

11. Read verses 12 to 16. What kind of picture do these verses paint of God? Do you see God in this way?

12. Memorise verse 17.

13. Paraphrase verses 18 and 19.

14. What verse or verses speak to you the most and why?

Answers

1. Paul the Apostle.

2. Probably somewhere between AD 61 and AD 63.

3. Probably Nicopolis.

4. Timothy.

5. To instruct Timothy to deal with false teachers and all areas of church life.

6. i) He is warning Timothy about false teachers of the law (verses 3 to 11).

   ii) Through his testimony of God's grace to him, he is encouraging Timothy to hold on to God and win the spiritual battles ahead (verses 12 to 20).

7. To stay in Ephesus and build up the church. To command certain men not to teach false doctrines.

8. By doing the following things:

   i) Submitting to those in leadership over you in Christ (pastor, etc.).

   ii) Reading and studying Scripture. God will never contradict His Word.

   iii) Being careful not to take one piece of Scripture out of context.

iv) Keeping close to God and obeying Him.

9. Righteousness; godliness; faith; love; endurance; gentleness—in fact all the characteristics of Jesus.

10. To preach the gospel. At his conversion—Acts 9:1–19 (see verses 15 to 16). Also recorded in Acts 22:21 and Acts 26:15–18.

11. i) A generous, giving, loving God. A God who is willing to give everything so that I could come into a friendship with Him. A God who is full of grace and mercy. A God who has *time* for me! Hallelujah!

    ii) Yes—I see God in this way although I constantly need to be reminded just how much love and concern He has for me. Reading these verses has made me see again what a brilliant Heavenly Father I have.

12. Now to the King eternal, immortal, invisible, the only God, be honour and glory for ever and ever. Amen.

13. Verses 18 to 19. I am reminding you through these instructions, Timothy my dear friend, whom I regard as my son, of God's word to you in the past. Follow the things I have told you and they will help you overcome the spiritual battles ahead. Cling on tight to your faith and keep a good conscience before God and men. Some people have turned away from these and have therefore lost and damaged their faith.

14. Verse 18. It's so easy to get bogged down with the worries and concerns in this life that I can easily take my eyes off God and forget God's promises to me. This verse tells Timothy to live by prophecies made about his life and by following them he will win the spiritual battles in this life. This verse encourages me to believe all that God has spoken to me in the past—and to live according to His Word now!

How to Memorise

You will find I ask you to memorise Scripture quite a lot. There are many reasons why we should memorise Scripture besides the fact that God has instructed us to do so (Deuteronomy 11:18). I have found it extremely helpful in witnessing and also in finding God's direction and guidance for my life, but most of all it really helps in moments of weakness or temptation. Notice what Jesus does when Satan tempts Him—He quotes Scripture (Matthew 4:4). When the enemy comes to condemn— God's Word is sharper than a two-edged sword (Hebrews 4:12).

Exercise Your Memory Banks!

Many people tell me that their memory is bad, but your memory can be trained to retain information. When I was young my parents sent me to speech and drama lessons. As well as developing me in the area of public speaking, it also had a tremendous effect on my memory! I had to memorise huge portions of Shakespeare and just loads of poems. The way I used to do it might help you. I would read the script over and over again—out loud preferably. Then, I would read it into a tape machine many times and in my spare time listen to it. I would leave it playing even when I was doing other things. Then I would break it down into portions: learn the first portion, then the first and second portions together, and so on. Then, I would try and say it without looking at the script. When I had memorised it all, I would say it over and over again until it became part of me. It's amazing what I can remember and recite from years and years ago. The mind is an extraordinary thing—once you have memorised something, it often stays. Let's take Galatians 2:20 for an example.

> *I have been crucified with Christ and I no longer live, but Christ lives in me. The life I live in the body, I live by faith in the Son of God, who loved me and gave himself for me.*

Let's take the first phrase: 'I have been crucified with Christ and I no longer live.' I would read that over and over again until I knew it, then I would add the second phrase: 'but Christ lives in me.' Then learn the first and second phrases together before adding the third: 'The life I live in the body'. Again I would say the three phrases over and over before adding the fourth: 'I live by faith in the Son of God'. After doing the same again, then add the fifth: 'who loved me and gave himself for me.' It's so much easier when you break it down into phrases. Also, it might help you to write your verse on a little card and review it during the day—or on your walk. Revision is so important, because being able to 'say' the verse doesn't actually mean you've memorised it—it needs reviewing so that it's imprinted in your memory banks.

How to Paraphrase

Many people have never attempted to paraphrase the Bible and yet it is such a great way of getting to grips with what the Bible is really saying. Paraphrasing is simply using your own words to express the meaning of the passage. During my years in Heartbeat, I discovered that some of the team found it very easy and helpful, whereas others struggled at the beginning. If you are one of those who find it difficult, may I encourage you to press on and discover how helpful paraphrasing can be.

To help you with your programmes, here is an example of paraphrasing.

Let's read Romans 10:10 in the NIV.

> *For it is with your heart that you believe and are justified, and it is with your mouth that you confess and are saved.*

Here's what it says in the Living Bible, which is a paraphrase of the Bible.

> *For it is by believing in his heart that a man becomes right with God; and with his mouth he tells others of his faith, confirming his salvation.*

Here's *my* paraphrase. Hope it helps you!

> *For if you believe in Jesus and all that He has done for you in your innermost being, that results in you being made right with God, and if you openly speak out your commitment to Christ then you are rescued.*

How to Write a Psalm

Throughout the years in team life, we have tried to be creative in the way we express our praise and worship to God. One of the ways we expressed our praise was in writing a psalm. It didn't matter if we hadn't written a song or poem before—everyone, musical or non-musical, was encouraged to take part. I found that as I put pen to paper a great explosion of praise to God seemed to take place within me. I'm sure that many of you have never written a psalm to God; however, I would encourage you to step out and put the praise in your heart into words. Do remember God looks on the heart, and not necessarily on how flowery your words are. Don't feel inadequate— everyone can do it. Just take up your pen and concentrate on your Heavenly Father—allow praise to well up within you and start writing. Here's a psalm I've recently written to God.

> *I will praise You, O Lord, as long as I live,*
> *because You alone are worthy!*
> *I know You surround me with Your love,*
> *I know You care for me like no other.*
> *You know all my faults,*
> *You know all there is to know about me*
> *and yet You still care.*
> *How can I fail to love You?*
> *My whole being cries out for You.*
> *Come close to me, O God.*
> *I am not satisfied with anything less than*
>   *Your love.*
> *I will praise You, O Lord, as long as I live,*
> *because You alone are worthy.*

CHAPTER 6

THE MEDITATION WORKOUT

What is meditation? It sounds dodgy, doesn't it?—like something out of an Eastern religion! Don't worry, it's got nothing to do with Transcendental Meditation or the New Age movement. It's completely biblical! There are many references regarding meditation in the Bible. Here are some that you can look up for yourself.

- Psalm 119:15
- Psalm 19:14
- Joshua 1:8
- Psalm 119:97
- Genesis 24:63
- Psalm 1:2
- Psalm 104:34

Paul Y. Cho says, in *Prayer:Key to Revival* (Word Books):

> Meditation is the act of contemplating or reflecting on something or someone. It demands discipline, since the mind tends to wander on many different things. It is an integral and important form of prayer. Since our actions are affected by our will and since the will is to a great degree affected by our

thinking (contemplation), we can control our actions.

Transcendental Meditation tells you to empty your mind—Christian meditation is allowing God and Scripture to fill your mind.

The first time I heard about meditation was at a conference in 1981. Alex Buchanan was the speaker and he asked us all to meditate on part of John 1:14, 'Jesus . . . full of grace and truth' and then share what we got. I remember thinking, 'I hope he doesn't pick me—I haven't a clue what he's talking about', but I tried with all my might to look as if I did! There was silence for about three minutes, then a well-known evangelist, a good friend of mine, spoke out and said, 'Alex, I'm sure I'm speaking for loads of people here, but I really don't know what to do.' Praise God for his honesty and courage! Alex then took us step by step into meditation. Since that time I've used it many times in my personal devotions and have found it a wonderful way of learning what God wants to teach us through His Word.

Some Helpful Steps

* Look up Romans 8:1.
* Ask God to speak to you through it.
* Read it through several times.
* Spend time thinking about what it says—allow the words to be absorbed into your mind.
* Perhaps dwell on a phrase or section of the verse.
* Allow yourself to follow a train of thought until you see something in this verse you've never seen before.
* Write down what you get.

• If your mind begins to wander completely off the subject, then read the Scripture again and focus your mind on the verse or verses.

I have personally used Romans 8:1 for meditation and I thought it might be helpful to share with you what God said. The first thing that struck me was the phrase, 'those who are in Christ Jesus'. I allowed my thoughts to dwell on the phrase for some time. Often we are taught that Jesus lives in us—but really it is, 'I in Him and He in me!' (1 John 4:13). I am in Christ Jesus, I am part of His body, the church—part of His family. I am in Him! I dwelt on this for some time and asked myself how being in Him makes me feel. It makes me feel protected, loved, part of Him, no longer belonging to myself, but part of Jesus' body—the church! It made me feel that any spiritual attack against me would be ineffective as the attacker would have to battle with Jesus first. I was completely surrounded by Jesus and felt completely protected as long as I remained in Him.

When you get the hang of it, you will want to meditate more and more. I often read a phrase or verse from Scripture in the morning and take it with me wherever I am going. In my few spare moments during the day, I turn it over in my mind, allow it to take root and meditate on it. It's a great way of allowing God's Word to sink deep into our innermost beings.

It's very easy, as you can see, and you'll find it a very releasing and fulfilling way of learning from God. Go for it! You'll enjoy it!

CHAPTER 7

THE PRAISE AND WORSHIP WORKOUT

One of the important things God said to us as we formed our first team, Heartbeat, in 1981 was that we should live out of a worship life together. One of our main priorities was to worship the Lord. Our teams have heard Ray and me say again and again that what we are with God on our own, is what we are when we come together as a team, and what we are as a team, is what we are when we go out to minister. We cannot suddenly change from what we are into some superspiritual being just by going on to a public platform. If we do—then God is not honoured and we are deceiving ourselves as well as the audience. We must develop an intimate friendship with God and spend time with Him in worship. It's so important.

We were created to worship God. 'Worship the Lord your God and serve Him only'(Matthew 4:10). God promises us blessings if we worship Him in spirit and in truth (Exodus 23:25). However, we should never worship God in order to gain something ourselves. We live in a world where people are always looking to what they can gain out of everything. Even although God blesses us, our main motivation must be selflessly giving ourselves to God because He deserves it. Our Heavenly Father has such a loving nature and therefore He wants to bless us over and over again. However, this should never be our motivation for worship.

I've noticed in many prayer meetings, when I have asked people to pray about issues or situations, quite a number of people pray; however, when I ask people to spend time praising God for who He is, few people actually pray. I have, therefore, come to the conclusion that some people find it difficult to express their praise and worship to God. We are not in the habit of praising one another and so it's often difficult to praise God. We know how to complain, but how do we praise Him?

You will find that I often start my programmes by asking you to look at a Psalm or a piece of Scripture that encourages you to praise the Lord. It's so important, before we begin each day with all its concerns and challenges, that we fix our eyes and thoughts on God. Reading a portion of Scripture helps us to do just that. David is a wonderful example. Even in the midst of horrendous difficulties, he still praised the Lord (Psalm 42:9–11, Psalm 52, Psalm 71:9–14). Job too continued to praise God even although everything went wrong and there seemed no explanation for what was happening (Job 13:15). I know from my own experience when situations or problems are weighing me down, it's often difficult to praise God, yet as I've dragged my mind off my concerns and started to praise God for who He is, it's as if the sun starts shining and the clouds disappear. When I focus my attention on my wonderful heavenly Father, my problems get into perspective.

A good example of this happened a number of years

ago when Heartbeat was invited to do a schools mission in a certain town in Britain. We had ten of the team with us and so we descended on the town in our van, minibus and car. The organisers promised to meet our costs and give us a gift over and above to help with our living costs. We had a very successful week visiting numerous schools, colleges and youth clubs. We worked hard and extremely long days. At the end of the week we were exhausted, but rejoicing at the many people who had become Christians.

The organisers were thrilled with the mission and as we left they handed us an envelope which contained their promised gift and expenses. On the way home, I opened the envelope, to receive quite a shock! The money didn't even cover the petrol, let alone any money to help with our living costs. As we drove home, anger and frustration began to flood my whole being. They knew how much our costs were and they weren't a small church, so why did they treat us so badly? It was then I asked Ray to put on a praise tape. I decided the only way to handle it was to praise God and not allow my anger and worries to cloud the journey. When we reached home, I still didn't feel what the organisers did was right, but I had got my eyes on God, on what He had done throughout the week and on how He promises to bless those who serve Him. Although it wasn't easy, it did change my heart and attitude and helped me forgive and not hold any grudges against those people.

It's so important to praise God. Why not try reading a Psalm each day? David's encouraging yet honest Psalms will, I'm sure, really bless you. Perhaps try writing down your praises to God and then read them aloud to Him. Don't just restrict your praise to Sundays or celebration meetings—dance, shout, sing, jump, raise hands, have your own praise party right there in your own room. I sometimes use a praise tape (see Appendix 2) to help me praise God by myself. Tell Him you love Him. Tell Him how much He is worth. Cultivate a praising heart—it will change your outlook on so many things! God is worth it.

Some Biblical Ways to Express Praise and Worship

1. Singing	Colossians 3:16
2. Singing a new song	Psalm 96:1
3. Singing in the Spirit	1 Corinthians 14:15
4. Dancing	Psalm 150:4
	2 Samuel 6:14–15
5. Clapping hands	Psalm 47:1
6. Kneeling	Psalm 95:6–7
7. Raising hands	Psalm 134:2
	1 Timothy 2:8
8. Shouting	Ezra 3:10–15
9. Speaking	Psalm 145:6–7
10. Standing	2 Chronicles 20:19
11. Bowing	2 Chronicles 20:18
	Matthew 2:11
	Nehemiah 8:6
12. Lying prostrate	Revelation 5:14
	Revelation 11:16
13. Playing an instrument in worship	Psalm 150:3–5
14. Leaping/jumping	Acts 3:8
15. Being still	Psalm 46:10

Being creative in your worship can really help bring life and a new sense of freedom in your relationship with God. Do try and use these different ways to worship Him. It's worth saying that it's not the ways in themselves that are worship, but that they are only the outward expression of something that's real inside us. We love God, therefore we raise hands, dance, sing, clap, etc. using our bodies to express our worship.

Hindrances to Worship

There are many different reasons why we might find it difficult to worship God. I've made a list of some of the most common hindrances I've come across. Why not read through them and see if you can identify any in yourself?

1. Fear	2 Timothy 1:7
2. Pride	Psalm 101:5
3. Pressure from others to conform	Romans 12:2
4. Sin	Matthew 6:14–15
5. Dry or dull spiritual life	Ephesians 5:18
6. Lack of or wrong teaching	John 8:31–32
7. Culture	Matthew 15:8–9
8. Rejection (or lack of self-worth)	1 Peter 2:4
9. Worry/problems at home/ work	1 Peter 5:7
10. Wrong concept of God	Matthew 7:11; John 3:16

If you can identify with any of these hindrances, it may be helpful not only to ask God to help you remove them, but also to pray with someone you respect in God. It is so important that we remove any blockages, so that we can worship Him. Someone once said, 'If you don't worship God, you don't worship nothing, you worship anything.' We were made to worship. Let's make sure it is God who gets our worship.

CHAPTER 8

THE PROGRAMMES

Programme 1

9.00–9.30   Read Psalm 37:1–6. Write out these verses in full. Underline the verses that speak to you most. Spend time praying about what God says to you through these verses.

9.30–11.00   Bible Study 1.

11.00–11.15   Drink and rest.

11.15–11.45   Go for a walk. Memorise Philippians 4:13 as you walk.

11.45–12.30   Read Proverbs 3:1–10 three times.
1. Paraphrase the whole section.
2. Memorise verses 5 and 6.
3. What is trust? Define the meaning. (Use dictionary, concordance, etc.)
4. What areas of trust do you find difficult?
5. Do you find it easy/hard to trust God? And why?
6. Do you find it easy/hard to trust others? And why?
7. Write down each blessing God promises through this passage of Scripture.
8. Spend the remaining time praying. Ask

12.30–1.30	Drink and rest.
1.30–3.00	Bible Study 2.
3.00–3.15	Drink and rest.

God to increase your level of trust in Him and in others.

3.15–3.45 Read Isaiah 25:9 (NIV). Thank God for His faithfulness. Spend time praising God for all His faithfulness to you. Use some biblical ways of expressing your praise, i.e. singing, clapping, dancing, shouting, kneeling, raising hands, etc. Try expressing your praise to God in ways you haven't used before. It might be good to use a praise tape (see Chapter 7 and Appendix 2).

3.45–4.30 There are many instructions in the Bible exhorting us to 'trust God'. There are many benefits from doing so. Look up each Scripture reference and see what God promises. Write out the verses in full.

- Psalm 22:4–5
- Psalm 32:10
- Psalm 37:5–6
- Psalm 56:3–4
- Psalm 25:2–3
- Psalm 37:3
- Psalm 40:4
- Proverbs 3:5–6

We are told in Scripture what we shouldn't put our trust in. Look up each of the following Scripture references to discover what we should not trust. Write out the verses in full.

- Psalm 44:6
- Psalm 146:3
- Jeremiah 48:7
- Psalm 49:5–7
- Jeremiah 17:5

Read Jeremiah 17:7–8. Meditate on this passage and write down what God says to you.

4.30–5.00   Spend some time repenting of the times when you've failed to trust God or others. Acknowledge your failure—then commit yourself to God. Imagine yourself on a road with God. Where you would like to be in the area of trust may seem many miles down the road—but all that God requires of you now is to take the first step. Put your hand into His and walk with Him. He'll be there to help you. (Taking a step forward with Him means trusting Him in situations you find difficult.)

Bible Study 1
2 Corinthians 1

Read the chapter at least three times.
1. Who wrote 2 Corinthians?
2. When was it written?
3. Where was it written?
4. To whom was it written?
5. What is he trying to communicate through this chapter?
6. Meditate on verses 3 and 4. Write down what God says to you.
7. If you have been hurt or damaged in your life, then read verse 5 again. What does it mean to have God's comfort in our lives? Has this happened to you? If not, why not?
8. Paraphrase verses 5, 6 and 7.

9. According to verse 9, why did Paul and his companions go through such trials and sufferings?
10. What does verse 10 teach us about Paul's trust in God? Could you trust God in similar circumstances?
11. How important was prayer to Paul?
12. Why does Paul go to lengths in verses 12 to 24 to explain his actions?
13. Memorise verse 20.
14. Write down any promises God has spoken to you. Declare your trust in God to fulfil each one just as His Word has said.
15. What does God do for us according to verses 21 and 22? Spend a couple of minutes thanking God for all He's done for you.

Bible Study 2
2 Corinthians 2

Read the chapter at least three times.
1. How can we stand firm in our walk with Christ?
2. How important is faith to God? Find a verse in Scripture that tells you.
3. What is Paul trying to communicate through this chapter?
4. How should we deal with a repentant sinner?
5. How important is it to forgive others? See Mark 11:25.
6. How easy/hard do you find it to forgive those who have hurt you? And why?
7. Meditate on verses 14 and 15. Write down what God says to you.
8. Paraphrase verses 14 to 17.

9. Verse 15 says we are the aroma of Christ. What does this mean?
10. What does it mean to 'peddle the word of God for profit'?
11. What verse/verses speak to you the most and why?

REMEMBER

> *When you finish do write me a letter.*

Mini Programme 1

30 minutes	Read Psalm 37:1–6. Write out these verses in full. Underline the verses that speak to you most. Spend time praying about what God says to you through these verses.
45 minutes	Read Proverbs 3:1–10 three times. 1. Paraphrase the whole section. 2. Memorise verses 5 and 6. 3. What is trust? Define the meaning. (Use dictionary, concordance, etc.). 4. What areas of trust do you find difficult? 5. Do you find it easy/hard to trust God? And why? 6. Do you find it easy/hard to trust others? And why? 7. Write down each blessing God promises through this passage of Scripture. 8. Spend the remaining time praying. Ask God to increase your level of trust in Him and in others.
30 minutes	Go for a walk. Memorise Philippians 4:13 as you walk.
30 minutes	Read Isaiah 25:9 (NIV). Thank God for His faithfulness. Praise God for all His faithfulness to you. Use some biblical ways of expressing your praise, i.e. singing, clapping, dancing, shouting, kneeling, raising hands, etc. Try expressing your praise to God in ways you haven't used before. It might be good to use a praise tape (see Chapter 7 and Appendix 2).

90 minutes   Bible Study No 1.

15 minutes   Go through all your notes. Write down what you have learned or what God has done in you today. Spend time repenting of the times you've failed to trust Him. Ask God to increase your faith in Him.

Programme 2

9.00–9.30	Read Psalm 27 twice. Write out specific verses that speak to you. Write down all that God says through this Psalm. Spend time in prayer thanking God for all He does for you.
9.30–11.00	Bible Study.
11.00–11.15	Drink and rest.
11.15–11.45	Answer the following questions:

1. Write down your feelings towards God.
2. Write down what kind of picture you have of God when you see Him as your Heavenly Father. Why do you see Him in this way?
3. What is your relationship like with your own father?
4. Do you feel any hurt or resentment towards your family? If so, why?

Spend time in prayer asking God to come and show you His Father's heart. Ask Him to show you how, throughout any hurt or despair in the past, He has been with you and has helped you even though you may not have known it. Ask God to help you to take down any barriers you have put up because of hurt or fear. Allow yourself to be loved and comforted by your Heavenly Dad. Write down all God says and does.

11.45–12.30	Go for a walk. Memorise these two verses as you walk.

- Hebrews 13:5—'*Never* will I leave you; *never* will I forsake you.'

- Psalm 145:13b—'The Lord is faithful to all his promises and loving towards all he has made.'

12.30–1.30	Drink and rest.
1.30–2.15	Read Isaiah 43.

1. There are many promises in this chapter. Write out each one.
2. Read verses 18 and 19. Write out on a piece of paper situations in the past that often haunt, bother or hurt you. Ask forgiveness for each one, if appropriate, then tear up the paper and throw it away, telling God that you choose to 'forget the former things'!
3. Spend time forgiving each person who has hurt you. (Much healing comes through forgiveness—even if you don't *feel* forgiveness, do it anyway as an act of obedience to God. Look up Matthew 5:44 and Mark 11:25.)
4. Spend time thanking God for the new things He is going to do with you. Thank Him for His presence through the good and the bad.

2.15–2.45 Read Zephaniah 3:7. Ask God how He feels about you. Write down what He says. Write down all the good things God has done for you throughout your life. Spend time praising God—use some biblical ways of expressing your praise, i.e. singing, clapping, dancing, shouting, kneeling, raising hands, etc. Try expressing your praise to God in ways you haven't used before. It might be a good idea to use a praise tape for this (see Chapter 7 and Appendix 2).

2.45–3.00   Drink and rest.

3.00–3.30   God has many aspects to His character—I've listed some of them here for you. Look up each Scripture reference and write out the verse in full.

1. Creator   Isaiah 40:28
2. Friend   Isaiah 41:8,
                 Proverbs 18:24
                 and John 15:14–15
3. Comforter   2 Corinthians 1:3
4. Counsellor   Isaiah 9:6
5. Protector   Psalm 91:2
                 and Psalm 121:7–8
6. Father   Psalm 68:5
                 and 2 Corinthians 6:18
7. Teacher   Isaiah 54:13
                 and John 14:26
8. Provider   Matthew 7:11

3.30–4.00   Go for a walk. Allow yourself to relax and enjoy walking with God. Imagine Him walking beside you. Ask Him if there's anything He wants to say to you while you walk together.

4.00–4.30   Read 1 John 3:1–3. Meditate on these verses and allow God to speak to you. Write down what He says.

4.30–5.00   Write down everything you have learned today. Spend time thanking God for being your Father. Commit yourself to Him for the future and allow His love to flood you.

Bible Study
Philemon

Read the book through three times (Don't faint—it's only one chapter long!)

1. Who wrote Philemon?
2. When was it written?
3. Where was it written?
4. To whom was it written?
5. What is the main purpose of this letter?
6. Read verses 4 and 5. What reasons did Paul give for always thanking God for the people to whom he was writing?
7. Read verse 5. How important is it for us to 'love the saints'? Find a verse in Scripture to back up your answer.
8. What does verse 6 mean?
9. When we love others, what does our love do to them according to verse 7?
10. Why should Philemon and the church perhaps not receive Onesimus? (You may have to look up a commentary for this answer.)
11. What kind of relationship did Paul have with Onesimus? See verses 10 to 12.
12. Read verses 8 to 19. Write down the kind of attitudes Paul displayed. What can we learn from this?
13. Read verse 18. This verse reminds us of a parable Jesus told. Which one and where is it found in Scripture?
14. Write down the main things you received from the Lord through this book.

Mini Programme 2

30 minutes   Read Psalm 27 twice. Write out specific verses that speak to you. Write down all that God says through this Psalm. Spend time in prayer thanking God for all He does for you.

30 minutes   Answer the following questions:
1. Write down your feelings towards God.
2. Write down what kind of picture you have of God when you see Him as your Heavenly Father. Why do you see Him in this way?
3. What is your relationship like with your own father?
4. Do you feel any hurt or resentment towards your family? If so, why?

Spend time in prayer asking God to come and show you His Father's heart. Ask Him to show you how, throughout any hurt or despair in the past, He has been with you and has helped you even though you may not have known it. Ask God to help you to take down any barriers you have put up because of hurt or fear. Allow yourself to be loved and comforted by your Heavenly Dad. Write down all God says and does.

15 minutes   Go for a walk. Memorise these two verses as you walk.

- Hebrews 13:5—'*Never* will I leave you; *never* will I forsake you.'

• Psalm 145:13b—'The Lord is faithful to all his promises and loving towards all he has made.'

45 minutes — Read Isaiah 43.
1. There are many promises in this chapter. Write out each one.
2. Read verses 18 and 19. Write out on a piece of paper situations in the past that often haunt, bother or hurt you. Ask forgiveness for each one, if appropriate, then tear up the paper and throw it away, telling God that you choose to 'forget the former things!'
3. Spend time forgiving each person who has hurt you. (Much healing comes through forgiveness—even if you don't *feel* forgiveness, do it anyway as an act of obedience to God. Look up Matthew 5:44 and Mark 11:25.)
4. Spend time thanking God for the new things He is going to do with you. Thank Him for His presence through the good and the bad.

90 minutes — Bible Study.

30 minutes — Write down everything you feel you have learned today. Spend time thanking God for being your Father. Commit yourself to Him for the future and allow His love to flood you.

Programme 3

9.00–9.15   Write down any specific aims you may have in spending this time with God and ask Him to begin to fulfil them in you today.

9.15–9.45   Read Psalm 46. Write down what God says to you through this chapter. Spend time praising God for who He is and for all He does for you.

9.45–11.15   Bible Study.

11.15–11.30 Drink and rest.

11.30–12.00 Go for a walk. Memorise John 14:1 as you walk.

12.00–12.30 Answer the following questions:

1. How did you became a Christian? Write out your story.
2. How easy/hard do you find witnessing to others? Give reasons for your answer.
3. How easy/hard do you find talking to God? Give reasons for your answer.
4. How easy/hard do you find listening to God? Give reasons for your answer.
5. How do you cope with bad news?
6. Do you tend to be a pessimist or an optimist? How does your answer affect your walk with God?
7. What is faith and how do we exercise it practically? Find a verse in the Bible that tells you what faith is.

12.30–1.30   Drink and rest.

1.30–1.45   Read and meditate on Romans 10:9–11. Write down what you get.

76

1.45–2.15 Look up the following references. Write down what happens when people believe and do not doubt.

- Mark 5
- Matthew 21:18–22
- John 11:17–44
- Mark 9:20–25
- Matthew 8:5–13
- 1 Peter 2:6

Declare your faith and trust in God to fulfil all His promises. Look up 1 Thessalonians 5:24. Write out the verse in full. Paraphrase the verse. Spend time praising God for His faithfulness.

2.15–2.45 Write down the meaning of the word 'doubt', as found in a dictionary. Read John 20:24–31.
1. How does Jesus deal with doubt?
2. What is His promise to us who believe yet have not seen?
3. Write down the areas where you find it difficult to trust and easy to doubt.
4. Try and assess why you find it difficult to trust in these areas.
5. What does the Bible say about someone who doubts? Look at James 1:6 and 7.
6. Ask God's forgiveness for your lack of faith and ask Him to increase your faith.

2.45–3.00 Drink and rest.
3.00–3.30 Go for a walk. Thank God for who He is and what He's done for you as you walk.
3.30–4.00 Look up Philippians 4:13 and Hebrews 13:5b. Write down the things you find difficult in your Christian life. Go through

	each one with God, speaking out these verses into each situation. Spend five minutes allowing God to speak to you. Write down what He says. Ask God to fill you with His Holy Spirit and declare your faith and trust in Him.
4.00–4.30	Write down all the good things God has done in your life. Spend time praising God for all He's done for you. Use some biblical ways of expressing your praise to God, i.e. singing, clapping, dancing, shouting, kneeling, raising hands, etc. It might be good to use a praise tape for this (see Chapter 7 and Appendix 2).
4.30–5.00	Go through all your notes. Write down what you have learned or what God has done throughout today. Thank God for all He has accomplished.

Bible Study
Acts 3—4:31

Read the passage at least three times.
1. Who wrote the book of Acts?
2. When was it written?
3. To whom was it written? And why?
4. Compare Peter and John's behaviour in these two chapters to how they behaved in Mark 14:43–72 and John 20:19. What was the difference? What had made them so bold?
5. Peter and John use every opportunity to share the good news about Jesus with the crowds. How do you feel about sharing your faith with others? And why?
6. Spend time asking God to forgive you for missed

opportunities that come to mind and ask God to enable you to speak with great boldness. See Acts 4:29.

7. The consequence of Peter and John's witness and preaching on this occasion and others was being thrown in jail. What was their response to this? See Acts 5:41–42.

8. We may not be persecuted in this way, but we may 'suffer' in other ways, e.g. be laughed at, scorned, made to look a fool, ignored, etc. How do you cope with these things?

9. Why did the high priest and Sadducees have problems with the beggar being healed?

10. Memorise Acts 4:12.

11. Read Acts 4:13. Write down what the Lord says to you through this verse.

12. Acts 4:11 and 25–26 quote Old Testament Scripture. Where can you find these verses in the Old Testament?

REMEMBER

> *Have you answered all the questions?*

Mini Programme 3

15 minutes	Write down any specific aims you may have in spending this time with God and ask Him to begin to fulfil them in you today.
30 minutes	Read Psalm 46. Write down what God says to you through this chapter. Spend time praising God for who He is and for all He does for you.
30 minutes	Write down the meaning of the word 'doubt', as found in a dictionary. Read John 20:24–31.

1. How does Jesus deal with doubt?
2. What is His promise to us who believe yet have not seen?
3. Write down the areas where you find it difficult to trust and easy to doubt.
4. Try and assess why you find it difficult to trust in these areas.
5. What does the Bible say about someone who doubts? Look at James 1:6 and 7.
6. Ask God's forgiveness for your lack of faith and ask Him to increase your faith.

15 minutes	Go for a walk. Memorise John 14:1 as you walk.
30 minutes	Look up the following references. Write down what happens when people believe and do not doubt.

- Mark 5
- Matthew 21:18–22
- John 11:17–44
- Mark 9:20–25
- Matthew 8:5–13
- 1 Peter 2:6

Declare your faith and trust in God to fulfil all His promises. Look up 1 Thessalonians 5:24. Write down what it says. Praise God for His faithfulness.

90 minutes   Bible Study.

30 minutes   Look up Philippians 4:13 and Hebrews 13:5b. Write down the things you find difficult in your Christian life. Go through each one with God, speaking out these verses into each situation. Spend five minutes allowing God to speak to you. Write down what He says. Ask God to fill you with His Holy Spirit and declare your faith and trust in Him.

Programme 4

9.00–9.15	Write down any specific aims you may have in spending this time with God and ask Him to begin to fulfil them in you today.
9.15–9.45	Read 2 Corinthians 4. Write down what God says to you through this chapter. Make a list of the things that Paul went through, i.e. shipwreck, etc. (see 2 Corinthians 11:23–28), and note that he was still able to praise God. Spend some time praying. Base your prayer on chapter 4, verses 16 to 18. Speak out your confidence in God to help you through any difficulties in your life.
9.45–10.15	Go for a walk. Memorise 1 Thessalonians 5:16–18 as you walk.
10.15–10.30	Drink and rest.
10.30–12.00	Bible Study 1.
12.00–12.30	Read James 1:2–4. According to these verses:

1. How should we face trials?
2. Why?
3. How do we become mature and complete in God?
4. Ask God to speak to you through these verses. Write down what He says.

12.30–1.30	Drink and rest.
1.30–2.00	

1. Pray and ask God how He feels about you and what He thinks of you. Write down His reply.
2. Find ten verses in the Bible that speak of God's love for us. Write down each reference.

82

3. Read Psalm 108:1–5. King David expresses his love and praise for God in this Psalm. Write a psalm expressing your love for God. Read it out loud to God. (See my example of a psalm on page 52.)

2.00–3.30 Bible Study 2.

3.30–3.45 Drink and rest.

3.45–4.15 Spend time writing down all the things God has done for you (small and big). Spend time praising God for all He's done for you. Use some biblical ways of expressing your praise, i.e. singing, clapping, dancing, shouting, kneeling, raising hands, etc. Try expressing your praise to God in ways you haven't used before. It might be good to use a praise tape for this (see Chapter 7 and Appendix 2).

4.15–4.45
1. Read John 17. Jesus prays for three things:
    a) Himself
    b) His disciples
    c) all believers.
2. Write down your own prayer to God about the following three things:
    a) yourself
    b) your friends/family
    c) the church worldwide.
3. Pray for five minutes, focusing on your family and friends—especially those who aren't yet Christians.

4.45–5.15
1. Meditate on Hebrews 3:13. Write down what God says to you.

83

2. What does it mean to encourage each other?
3a. Ask God to show you ways in which you could practically encourage your family over the next few days. Write them down and give yourself a time limit to do the things God gives you.
3b. Ask God to show you ways in which you could practically encourage your friends over the next few days. Write them down and give yourself a time limit to do the things God gives you.

5.15–5.30 Look over all your notes taken today. In the light of discovering or rediscovering how much God loves you, take some time to commit yourself to going forward into the future with God, no matter how much it costs. Perhaps write down your commitment on paper before God.

Bible Study 1
Genesis 37 and 39

Read each chapter at least three times.
1. Who wrote Genesis?
2. Who were Joseph's father and mother?
3. Are his mother and father alive at this point in the story?
4. Joseph's brothers were jealous of Joseph. Why?
5. Describe the emotions Joseph must have felt when his brothers tied him up and put him in a pit.
6. His brothers then sold him into slavery for 20 shekels. How would Joseph feel knowing he would perhaps never see his father, brothers or home again?

7. What did God do to help Joseph? See chapter 39, verses 2 to 6.
8. Read verses 7 to 12. How does Joseph react when tempted sexually? What can you learn from this?
9. Read verses 13 to 20. Joseph is wrongly accused. How do you think he felt?
10. Read verses 20 to 23. Again, what did God do for Joseph?
11. God was with Joseph throughout all his trials—take time to thank Him for doing the same for you.
12. After all the rejection, loneliness, etc. that Joseph experienced, did he react against his brothers—or did he forgive them? Read Genesis 50:15–21. Write down Joseph's reaction to his brothers. How does this speak to you?

Bible Study 2
Romans 15

Read the chapter at least three times.
1. Who wrote Romans?
2. When was it written?
3. Where was it written?
4. To whom was it written?
5. Paraphrase verses 1 to 5.
6. In what practical way can you carry out the instruction of verses 1 and 2?
7. Read verse 5. Where else in Scripture does Jesus pray for us to have unity?
8. Memorise verse 6.
9. Why is unity so important to God and to His plans for us and His Kingdom?
10. Verse 7 tells us to accept each other just as Christ

accepts us—faults included! How easy/hard is it for you to do this and why?

11. Read verse 8. Write down a verse or verses in Scripture that shows Jesus as a servant.

12. Read verse 13. What happens as you trust in God?

13. Read verses 15 and 16. Paul knows his calling and repeats it through Scripture again and again. In what passage of Scripture does God tell Paul what He wants him to do?

14. Meditate on verse 17. Write down what you get.

15. Write down what you believe God has called you to do.

16. Verse 20 explains Paul's ambition to preach where Christ was not known. What is the difference between worldly ambition and spiritual ambition? How can we make sure we are not following worldly ambition?

17. Read verse 25. What happened when Paul reached Jerusalem with the offering for the saints?

18. What are the main things that God has said to you through this chapter?

REMEMBER ▶ *If you are unsure how to paraphrase/ meditate/study/write a psalm etc., then do refer to the appropriate chapter.*

Mini Programme 4

15 minutes   Write down any specific aims you may have in spending this time with God and ask Him to begin to fulfil them in you today.

30 minutes   Read 2 Corinthians 4. Write down what God says to you through this chapter. Make a list of the things that Paul went through, i.e. shipwreck, etc. (see 2 Corinthians 11:23–28), and note that he was still able to praise God. Spend some time praying. Base your prayer on chapter 4, verses 16 to 18. Speak out your confidence in God to help you through any difficulties.

15 minutes   Go for a short walk. Memorise 1 Thessalonians 5:16–18 as you walk.

30 minutes   Read James 1:2–4. According to these verses:
1. How should we face trials?
2. Why?
3. How do we become mature and complete in God?
4. Ask God to speak to you through these verses. Write down what He says.

30 minutes
1. Pray and ask God how He feels about you and what He thinks of you. Write down His reply.
2. Find ten verses in the Bible that speak of God's love for us. Write down each reference.
3. Read Psalm 108:1–5. King David expresses his love and praise for God in this Psalm. Write a psalm expressing

	your love for God. Read it out loud to God. (See my example of a psalm on page 52.)
90 minutes	Bible Study 1.
15 minutes	Spend time writing down all the things God has done for you (small and big). Spend time praising God for all He's done for you. Use some biblical ways of expressing your praise, i.e. singing, clapping, dancing, shouting, kneeling, raising hands, etc. Try expressing your praise to God in ways you haven't used before. It might be good to use a praise tape for this (see Chapter 7 and Appendix 2).
15 minutes	Look over all your notes taken today. In the light of discovering or rediscovering how much God loves you, take some time to commit yourself to going forward into the future with God, no matter how much it costs. Perhaps write down your commitment on paper before God.

Programme 5

9.00–9.30	Read Psalm 146. Write down what God says to you through this chapter and spend time in prayer and praise thereafter.
9.30–11.00	Bible Study 1.
11.00–11.15	Drink and rest.
11.15–11.45	Go for a walk. Meditate on and memorise Philippians 4:6 as you walk.
11.45–12.30	Read Luke 10:38–42. Answer the following questions:

    1. Why was Martha so upset, annoyed and worried?
    2. Why did Jesus say that Mary chose the better way?
    3. Can you identify with Martha?
    4. What can you learn from this story?

Read Luke 12:22–31. Answer the following questions:

    1. List all the things Jesus tells us not to worry about.
    2. Verse 24. Do you consider yourself valuable to God? If not, why not?
    3. What is the opposite of worry?
    4. How do we practically 'seek his Kingdom'?

Spend the remaining time praying about your answers.

12.30–1.30	Drink and rest.
1.30–3.00	Bible Study 2.
3.00–3.15	Drink and rest.
3.15–3.45	The evils of worry can be found in the following verses. Look up each Scripture

reference and write down what can happen when we worry.

- Matthew 13:22
- Matthew 6:25–32
- Luke 21:34

Now look up the following Scripture references. Write down what happens when we have faith.

- Acts 10:43
- John 12:36
- Ephesians 3:12
- Acts 2:18
- Acts 15:9
- John 20:31
- Romans 5:1

3.45–4.15 Read Matthew 11:28–30. Meditate on these verses. Ask God to speak to you through them. Write down what He says and pray thereafter.

4.15–4.30 Write down everything that concerns or worries you. Ask God to reveal to you why you are worried or concerned; ask for forgiveness for lack of trust, unbelief, etc. and give your worries to God. Declare your faith, and trust in God to work in your situation.

4.30–5.00 Spend an energetic time praising God. Thank God for all He's done in you today. Use some biblical ways, i.e. singing, clapping, dancing, shouting, kneeling, raising hands, etc. Try expressing your praise to God in ways you haven't used before. It might be good to use a praise tape for this (see Chapter 7 and Appendix 2).

Bible Study 1
Ephesians 1

Read the chapter at least three times.
1. Who wrote Ephesians?
2. When was it written?
3. Where was it written?
4. To whom was it written?
5. Write down a list of spiritual blessings we receive through Christ.
6. Read verse 4 again and make it personal, i.e. 'He chose me before . . .' Write down how that makes you feel.
7. What is predestination?
8. What does Paul keep praying for the Ephesians?
9. Paraphrase verses 18 to 21.
10. Which verse speaks to you the most and why? Memorise that verse.
11. What is Paul trying to communicate through this chapter?

Bible Study 2
Ephesians 2

Read the chapter at least three times.
1. Who is Paul talking about when he mentions in verse 2 'the ruler of the kingdom of the air'?
2. Verse 4 talks of God's great love for us. Find another verse in Scripture that talks of God's great love. Ask God to show you a picture of how great His love is for you. Spend a few minutes thanking Him for His great love.
3. Meditate on verse 6. Write down what God says.
4. Memorise verses 8 and 9.
5. Read verse 12. There was a time when you did not

know God and were 'without hope and without God in the world'. Pray for two friends who are still in that position and ask God to speak to them.

6. With so much worry and stress in our world today, it's great to read verse 14: 'For he himself is our peace.' Take time to thank God for the peace He gives you.

7. How many times is the word PEACE mentioned in the chapter?

8. This chapter talks a lot about us being 'fellow citizens with God's people and members of God's household' (see verse 19). How can we practically live in the world, but not be of this world?

9. What are the main things God has said to you through this chapter?

Mini Programme 5

30 minutes
Read Psalm 146. Write down what God says to you through this chapter and spend time in prayer and praise thereafter.

30 minutes
The evils of worry can be found in the following verses. Look up each Scripture reference and write down what can happen when we worry.

- Matthew 13:22   •Luke 21:34
- Matthew 6:25–32

Now look up the following Scripture references. Write down what happens when we have faith.

- Acts 10:43   • Acts 15:9
- John 12:36   • John 20:31
- Ephesians 3:12   • Romans 5:1
- Acts 2:18

45 minutes
Read Luke 10:38–42. Answer the following questions:
1. Why was Martha so upset, annoyed and worried?
2. Why did Jesus say that Mary chose the better way?
3. Can you identify with Martha?
4. What can you learn from this story?

Read Luke 12:22–31. Answer the following questions:
1. List all the things Jesus tells us not to worry about.

2. Verse 24. Do you consider yourself valuable to God? If not, why not?
3. What is the opposite of worry?
4. How do we practically 'seek his Kingdom'?

Spend the remaining time praying about your answers.

15 minutes	Go for a walk. Meditate on and memorise Philippians 4:6 as you walk.
90 minutes	Bible Study 1.
15 minutes	Write down everything that concerns or worries you. Ask God to reveal to you why you are worried or concerned; ask for forgiveness for lack of trust, unbelief, etc. and give your worries to God. Declare your faith, and trust in God to work in your situation.
15 minutes	Spend an energetic time praising God. Thank God for all He's done in you today. Use some biblical ways, i.e. singing, clapping, dancing, shouting, kneeling, raising hands, etc. Try expressing your praise to God in ways you haven't used before. It might be good to use a praise tape for this (see Chapter 7 and Appendix 2).

Programme 6

9.00–9.15	Write down any specific aims you may have in spending this time with God and ask Him to begin to fulfil them in you today.
9.15–9.45	Read 2 Peter 1. Write down what God says to you through this chapter. Spend some time praying thereafter.
9.45–11.15	Bible Study 1.
11.15–11.30	Drink and rest.
11.30–12.00	Go for a walk. As you walk thank God for Jesus and for your salvation.
12.00–12.30	Write down your natural giftings. Write each one on a separate piece of paper. Go through them one by one with God. Thank Him for each one and make a point of laying each one down. Tell Him He is more important to you than the gifts He gives you. Ask Him to 'put to death the desires of flesh', and to raise up only those giftings that He can use in His Kingdom. If you do this with all honesty and integrity, you will find this time to be significant in the months and years ahead.
12.30–1.30	Drink and rest.
1.30–3.00	Bible Study 2.
3.00–3.15	Drink and rest.
3.15–3.45	Read Philippians 2. Paul has given us several instructions in this chapter to make us more like Christ. Write down each instruction. Go through the list and note where you could improve your walk with God. Ask God to help you in each area.

3.45–4.00	Praise God for all He's doing in your life. Use some biblical ways of expressing your praise, i.e. singing, clapping, dancing, shouting, kneeling, raising hands, etc. Try expressing your praise to God in ways you haven't used before. It might be good to use a praise tape for this (see Chapter 7 and Appendix 2).
4.00–4.30	Ask God to speak to you through Scripture about the future direction of your life. Write down what He says. Also ask God what He wants you to be doing for Him right now. Write down areas in your church, home, school, work where you could serve God. Pray and ask God to open up these areas to you.
4.30–5.00	Read Joshua 1. Note how God encourages Joshua as he takes the leadership of the Israelites. Write down God's instructions to Joshua. What does God require of Joshua? Write down what you can learn from this chapter. Thank God for all the encouragement you have received and will receive from Him. Thank Him that He will be with you in the future each step of the way. (Matthew 28:20—'And surely I am with you *always*, to the very end of the age.')

Bible Study 1
Psalm 84

Read the Psalm at least three times.
1. Who wrote this Psalm?
2. Write down the main theme of this Psalm.

3. Meditate on verse 2. Write down what God says to you.
4. Verse 4 states that we are blessed if we dwell near God. How can we practically do this?
5. What does it mean to 'set your heart on pilgrimage'?
6. Paraphrase verses 10 and 11.
7. Memorise verse 10.
8. Verse 11 says, 'For the Lord God is a sun and shield.' Write down a list of good things that the sun does for us, and also the same for a shield, e.g. sun brings light, shield protects, etc. Then spend time thanking God that He does each one of these things for us!
9. Write out your own psalm, expressing your praise to God. (See my example of a psalm on page 52.)
10. Write down the main things God says to you through this Psalm.

Bible Study 2
Romans 12

Read the chapter at least three times.
1. Who wrote Romans?
2. When was it written?
3. Where was it written?
4. To whom was it written?
5. Read verse 1. What does it mean to offer your body as a living sacrifice?
6. Read verse 2. How can we practically renew our minds?
7. How do we discern God's will according to this chapter?
8. Verse 3 says we should have sober judgement of ourselves. Normally we either think of ourselves too highly, or we think we're not capable of anything at

all. We all fall into one of these categories more than the other. Which one would you naturally fall into and why? What can you do to 'have a sober judgement of yourself'?

9. Verse 9 says, 'Love must be sincere.' Look up 1 Corinthians 13 and list all the things that love should be, e.g. love is patient.

10. Read verse 10. How do we practically 'honour' others above ourself?

11. Memorise verse 12.

12. Verse 13 commands us to practise hospitality. How can we do this in our everyday lives—especially those who don't have their own homes?

13. Be honest! How easy/hard do you find verse 14? Where in Scripture does Jesus tell us we are blessed when people persecute us?

14. Read verse 19. What does this verse mean? Can you think of an example of this in Scripture? Give chapter and verse.

15. Read verse 20. What does it mean to 'heap burning coals on his head'? (You may need to use a commentary here.)

16. What verse(s) speak(s) to you the most and why?

REMEMBER *If you are on medication, please consult your doctor before fasting.*

Mini Programme 6

15 minutes	Write down any specific aims you may have in spending this time with God and ask Him to begin to fulfil them in you today.
30 minutes	Read 2 Peter 1. Write down what God says to you through this chapter. Then spend time praying thereafter.
15 minutes	Read Philippians 2. Paul has given us several instructions in this chapter to make us more like Christ. Write down each instruction. Go through the list and note where you could improve your walk with God. Pray and ask God to help you in each area.
15 minutes	Go for a walk. As you walk thank God for Jesus and for your salvation.
30 minutes	Write down your natural giftings. Write each one on a separate piece of paper. Go through them one by one with God. Thank Him for each one and make a point of laying each one down. Tell Him He is more important to you than the gifts He gives you. Ask Him to 'put to death the desires of flesh', and to raise up only those giftings that He can use in His Kingdom. If you do this with all honesty and integrity, you will find this time to be significant in the months and years ahead.
15 minutes	Praise God for all He's doing in your life. Use some biblical ways of expressing your praise, i.e. singing, clapping, dancing, shouting, kneeling, raising hands, etc. Try

	expressing your praise to God in ways you haven't used before. It might be good to use a praise tape for this (see Chapter 7 and Appendix 2).
90 minutes	Bible Study 1.
30 minutes	Ask God to speak to you through Scripture about the future direction of your life. Write down what He says. Also ask God what He wants you to be doing for Him right now. Write down areas in your church, home, school, work where you could serve God. Pray and ask God to open up these areas to you.

Programme 7

9.00–9.30	Read Psalm 145. Write down what God says to you through this Psalm and spend time in prayer and praise thereafter.
9.30–10.00	The Bible tells us to 'Worship the Lord your God and serve him only' (Matt. 4:10b).

1. What is 'worship'?
2. Write down ways in which you could express your worship to God. Try and find verses which show that way being used in the Bible.
3. How long per day do you normally spend worshipping God?
4. What would hinder you from worshipping God?

10.00–11.30	Bible Study 1.
11.30–11.45	Drink and rest.
11.45–12.00	Spend time worshipping God using some of the biblical ways to worship you've discovered above. Thank Him for all you've learned this morning. It might be good to use a worship tape (see Chapter 7 and Appendix 2).
12.00–12.30	Go for a walk. Thank God for all the beauty in nature around you as you walk.
12.30–1.30	Drink and rest.
1.30–3.00	Bible Study 2.
3.00–3.15	Drink and rest.
3.15–4.00	Read Mark 14:32—15:38.

1. Write down the number of times Jesus was rejected in this passage.

2. Write down the way you feel when others reject you.
3. Write down any hurts you have now or had in the past for which you need God's healing.
4. Why is it important to forgive those who hurt us?
5. Find a verse in Scripture that tells you forgiveness is important.
6. Thank God for all the love He has for you. Ask Him to heal any hurts or rejection you may have experienced. Forgive those who have hurt you and allow God to bring healing to you.

4.00–4.30 Go for a walk. Think of two people you find it difficult to get on with. Pray for them as you walk.

4.30–5.00 Read 1 Peter 1:13–16.
1. What does it mean to be holy? (Look up dictionary, concordance, etc. for meaning.)
2. How do you become holy?
3. Spend time asking God to give you a pure heart and mind.

5.00–6.00 Spend this time with your leader/counsellor/pastor or do the following:
1. Look through your notes. Write down what you have learned today.
2. Spend time praying about any areas of weakness. Praise God for all He's doing and will continue to do.

Bible Study 1
Colossians 1

Read the chapter at least three times.
1. Who wrote Colossians?
2. Where was it written and under what circumstances?
3. When was it written?
4. To whom was it written?
5. What is he trying to communicate through this chapter?
6. Read verses 3 to 5. What encouraged Paul about the brothers at Colosse?
7. Read verses 9 to 12. What does Paul pray for the Colossians?
8. Paraphrase verses 15 to 20.
9. What verse speaks to you the most and why?
10. Memorise that verse.
11. Read verses 21 to 23 again. Spend some time thanking Jesus for all He did for you on the cross.
12. In verse 25 Paul explains the commission God has given him—to preach the good news of God in its fullness. What is your commission? What task or tasks has God given you to do and what are you doing practically to outwork them?
13. Read verse 29. Write down what God says to you through this verse.

Bible Study 2
Colossians 2

Read the chapter at least three times.
1. Read verses 1 to 3. What does Paul want to see happen in the Colossians?

2. Paul talks about being 'encouraged in heart and united in love'. Why is unity so important to God? Find a verse to back up your answer.
3. Memorise verse 6.
4. How can we 'continue to live in Him, rooted and built up in Him, strengthened in faith as you were taught, and overflowing with thankfulness'? What practical things can we do to accomplish this?
5. Meditate on verses 9 and 10. Write down what God says to you.
6. Read verses 13 to 15. Write down what God has done for you according to these verses.
7. Read verse 20. Examine yourself and your lifestyle. Do you still submit in any way to the basic principles of the world? If so, spend some time talking to God about it.
8. What are the main points Paul is trying to communicate through this chapter?

Mini Programme 7

30 minutes	Read Psalm 145. Write down what God says to you through this Psalm and spend time in prayer and praise thereafter.
30 minutes	The Bible tells us to 'Worship the Lord your God and serve Him only'(Matt 4:10b).

1. What is 'worship'?
2. Write down ways in which you could express your worship to God. Try and find verses which show that way being used in the Bible.
3. How long per day do you normally spend worshipping God?
4. What would hinder you from worshipping God?

45 minutes   Read Mark 14:32—15:38.

1. Write down the number of times Jesus was rejected in this passage.
2. Write down the way you feel when others reject you.
3. Write down any hurts you have now or had in the past for which you need God's healing.
4. Why is it important to forgive those who hurt us?
5. Find a verse in Scripture that tells you forgiveness is important.
6. Thank God for all the love He has for you. Ask Him to heal any hurts or rejection you may have experienced. Forgive those who have hurt you and allow God to bring healing to you.

15 minutes   Spend time worshipping God using some

of the biblical ways to worship you've discovered above. Thank Him for all you've learned today. It might be good to use a worship tape (see Chapter 7 and Appendix 2).

90 minutes	Bible Study 1.
30 minutes	Spend this time with your leader/counsellor/pastor or do the following:

1. Look through your notes. Write down what you have learned today.
2. Spend time praying about any areas of weakness. Praise God for all He's doing and will continue to do.

Programme 8

Day One

9.00–9.15   Write down any specific aims you may have in spending this time with God and ask Him to begin to fulfil them in you over the next two days.

9.15–9.45   Read Psalm 139. Write down what God says to you through this Psalm. Write out in full the verses that God uses to speak to you.

9.45–11.15   Bible Study 1.

11.15–11.30   Drink and rest.

11.30–12.00   Go for a walk. Pick a leaf from a tree. Ask God to speak to you through it. Write down what He says.

12.00–12.30
a) Ask God how He feels about the following things (spend at least ten minutes on each subject):
    1. your nation
    2. the church in your nation.
b) Write down the visions, verses, words God gives you. Spend at least ten minutes praying for your nation. Ask God to forgive us for the wrong things going on in our nation at this time.
c) Do the same for the church in your nation.

12.30–1.30   Drink and rest.

1.30–2.00   Write down everything in your life that you can praise God for. Spend time praising God; use some biblical ways of expressing your praise, i.e. singing, clapping, dancing,

107

shouting, kneeling, raising hands, etc. Try expressing your praise to God in ways you haven't used before. It might be good to use a praise tape (see Chapter 7 and Appendix 2).

2.00–2.45   Read Colossians 1:15–23 twice. Answer the following questions:

1. How and when did you become a Christian?
2. What does Jesus mean to you?
3. Meditate on verse 17. Write down what you get.
4. Read verse 22. It says that you are 'holy in his sight, without blemish and free from accusation' because of Jesus' death. Write down how that makes you feel.
5. Write down what Jesus accomplished for you on the cross (i.e. forgiveness, freedom, etc.)
6. Write out a letter to God expressing your love and thankfulness to Him for all He's done for you.
7. Read your letter out loud to God and spend time thanking Him for all He's done for you.

2.45–3.00   Drink and rest.
3.00–5.00   Read some chapters from the book you have chosen from the list in Appendix 1.

Day Two

9.00–9.30   Read Psalm 91. Write down what God says

	to you through this Psalm. Spend time praying thereafter.
9.30–11.00	Bible Study 2.
11.00–11.15	Drink and rest.
11.15–11.45	Go for a walk. As you walk thank God for all the beauty you see around you, i.e. sun, sky, trees, etc.
11.45–12.30	Answer the following questions:

1. Do you feel loved by God? If not, why not?
2. Read Romans 5:6–8 and 1 John 4:9–10. Ask God to show you how much He loves you. Write down any verses of Scripture, visions, thoughts you might receive.
3. How could your friendship with God improve? What things could you do to make it improve?
4. Spend a few minutes telling God how much you love Him. Express your love for Him in a worship song; sit in silence in His presence at the end of your worship time. Allow His love to enfold you.
5. Write down any feelings, thoughts, etc. you had during your worship time.

12.30–1.30	Drink and rest.
1.30–3.00	Bible Study 3.
3.00–3.15	Drink and rest.
3.15–3.45	God has 'chosen' you to be part of His family and set you apart for work in His Kingdom.

1. Write down several Scripture references where it refers to us being 'chosen'.

2. Read Luke 6:12–16. What does this tell you about how Jesus chose His disciples?
3. Meditate on the fact that *you* are chosen! Write down how this makes you feel.

3.45–4.15
1. Read Luke 22 and 23. Pray out of your response to Jesus' love for you.
2. Read Luke 24. I would encourage you to commit yourself to going on with God and doing all that He would want you to do with your life.

4.15–5.30   Read some chapters from the book you have chosen from the list in Appendix 1.

5.30–6.00   Spend this time with your counsellor/pastor/leader or answer the following questions:
1. Write down what you are going to do differently in your walk with God because of the time you've spent over the last two days.
2. Write down in brief what you have learned over the last two days.
3. Spend time praying—committing yourself to a deeper walk with God.

Bible Study 1
1 John 1 and 2

Read the chapters at least three times.
1. Who wrote 1 John?
2. Where was it written?
3. When was it written?

4. To whom was it written?
5. Why was it written?
6. Paraphrase chapter 1, verses 6 to 10.
7. Memorise chapter 1, verse 9.
8. Write down all the things (sins) you've done wrong that you've never asked forgiveness for. Ask the Holy Spirit to highlight any sins or situations from the past. (Don't bring up 'old' sins for which God's already forgiven you—they are forgiven and forgotten!) Go through each one and ask God to forgive you. Then tear up the piece of paper and throw it in the rubbish bin! Spend time thanking God for His forgiveness.
9. Read chapter 2, verse 1. Who speaks to God on our behalf?
10. How, according to this passage, do we come to know Him?
11. Meditate on chapter 2, verses 9 to 11. Write down what God says to you.
12. What verse from these two chapters speaks to you the most and why?

Bible Study 2
1 John 3 and 4

Read the chapters at least three times.
1. Write out chapter 3, verse 1. When we become Christians, we are called 'children of God'. Ask God for a picture as to how He loves and treats His children. Write it down. Also write down how it makes you feel.
2. Read chapter 3, verse 10. Is there anyone in your family/friends that you do not get on with? Spend time

asking God to help you put the situation right. Spend time asking God to forgive you for any hardness of heart or unforgiving spirit. Determine yourself that you will show love even if the situation is not your fault. God will help you and give you the resources needed.

3. Read chapter 3, verse 23. What is God's command to us?
4. Pick a verse from the chapter and memorise it.
5. Chapter 4, verse 1—how can we 'test the spirits to see whether they are from God'?
6. How has God proved His love for us?
7. Find another verse elsewhere in Scripture that talks of God's love for us.
8. Do you love God? How do you show your love to Him? Think of more ways you can show your love to God.

Bible Study 3
1 John 5

Read the chapter three times.

1. Paraphrase verses 1 to 5.
2. Read verse 11. Meditate on this verse and write down what you get.
3. Think for a few minutes about your quality of life. Jesus says, 'I have come that you might have life and have it to the full.' In Jesus there is 'life to the full'. Is this what you are experiencing? If not, then list things that might hinder you from living that 'life to the full', e.g. money, etc.
4. Memorise verse 12.

5. Read verse 14. Have you got confidence in approaching God? If not, why not?
6. What should we do if we see another Christian do something wrong?
7. Write down the main points of this whole book. What is the author trying to communicate?

REMEMBER

Helps on hearing from God are on pages 39–43.

Mini Programme 8

Day One

15 minutes	Write down any specific aims you may have in spending this time with God and ask Him to begin to fulfil them in you over the next two days.
30 minutes	Read Psalm 139. Write down what God says to you through this Psalm. Write out in full the verses that God uses to speak to you.
15 minutes	Go for a walk. Pick a leaf from a tree. Ask God to speak to you through it. Write down what He says.
45 minutes	Read Colossians 1:15–23 twice. Answer the following questions: 1. How and when did you become a Christian? 2. What does Jesus mean to you? 3. Meditate on verse 17. Write down what you get. 4. Read verse 22. It says that you are 'holy in his sight, without blemish and free from accusation' because of Jesus' death. Write down how that makes you feel. 5. Write down what Jesus accomplished for you on the cross (i.e. forgiveness, freedom, etc.). 6. Write out a letter to God expressing your love and thankfulness to Him for all He's done for you. 7. Read your letter out loud to God and

	spend time thanking Him for all He's done for you.
90 minutes	Bible Study 1.
15 minutes	Write down everything in your life that you can praise God for. Spend time praising God; use some biblical ways of expressing your praise, i.e. clapping, dancing, singing, jumping, shouting, etc. Try expressing your praise to God in ways you haven't used before. It might be good to use a praise tape (see Chapter 7 and Appendix 2).
30 minutes	a) Ask God how He feels about the following things (spend at least ten minutes on each subject):
	1. your nation
	2. the church in your nation.
	b) Write down the visions, verses, words God gives you. Spend at least ten minutes praying for your nation. Ask God to forgive us for the wrong things going on in our nation at this time.
	c) Do the same for the church in your nation.

Day Two

30 minutes	Read Psalm 91. Write down what God says to you through this Psalm. Spend time praying thereafter.
30 minutes	God has 'chosen' you to be part of His family and set you apart for work in His Kingdom.
	1. Write down several Scripture references

115

where it refers to us being 'chosen'.

2. Read Luke 6:12–16. What does this tell you about how Jesus chose His disciples? Meditate on the fact that you are chosen! Write down how this makes you feel.

15 minutes Go for a walk. As you walk thank God for all the beauty you see around you, i.e. sun, sky, trees, etc.

45 minutes Answer the following questions:

1. Do you feel loved by God? If not, why not?

2. Read Romans 5:6–8 and 1 John 4:9–10. Ask God to show you how much He loves you. Write down any Scripture, visions, thoughts you might receive.

3. How could your friendship with God improve? What things could you do to make it improve?

4. Spend a few minutes telling God how much you love Him. Express your love for Him in a worship song; sit in silence in His presence at the end of your worship time. Allow His love to enfold you.

5. Write down any feelings, thoughts, etc. you had during your worship time.

90 minutes Bible Study 2.

30 minutes

1. Read Luke 22 and 23. Pray out of your response to Jesus' love for you.

2. Read Luke 24. I would encourage you to commit yourself to going on with God and doing all that He would want you to do with your life.

Programme 9

Day One

9.00–9.15	Write down any specific aims you may have in spending this time with God and ask Him to begin to fulfil them in you over the next two days.
9.15–9.45	Read Psalm 108. Pick out one verse and meditate on it. Write down what God says to you and spend time praying thereafter.
9.45–11.15	Bible Study 1.
11.15–11.30	Drink and rest.
11.30–12.00	Ask God how He feels about your nation. Allow Him to show you pictures/visions or lead you to Scriptures which reveal His heart. Ask Him to show you how much He loves your nation and to show you the compassion He has for the people of your land. Write down how He feels.
12.00–12.30	Go for a walk. As you walk pray for your nation. Pray for your nation's leader, the government, the opposition parties, people in charge of the media (TV, newspapers etc.), people in charge of education. Pray for righteousness and justice.
12.30–1.30	Drink and rest.
1.30–2.00	Answer the following questions:

1. What is the main priority in your life?
2. What are your aims in life?
3. What are you doing practically to fulfil these aims?
4. Write down the structure of a normal working day (24-hour structure).

5. Write down the structure of a normal day off.
6. How long do you normally spend in prayer each day?
7. How long do you normally spend in Bible study?
8. How often and how long do you watch television?
9. How long do you spend physically exercising?
10. How much time do you spend in church or at church meetings?
11. How much time do you spend per week in evangelism?

2.00–3.30   Bible Study 2.

3.30–3.45   Drink and rest.

3.45–4.00   Go through your answers to the questions above. Assess whether you are spending your time profitably for God's Kingdom. Are you spending too much time on television, video, etc. and not enough time in prayer? Are you fulfilling the aims you have for your life? Think of ways you can improve your lifestyle. Pray and ask God if there is anything He would like you to change. Write down what God says and if there are any changes then make sure you carry them out.

4.00–5.00   Read Daniel 9. Notice verses 3 to 19 in particular. This is Daniel's prayer to God on behalf of his nation. Write down your prayer to God about your nation, basing it on Daniel's prayer. Afterwards, spend some time repenting on behalf of your nation, asking God to bring revival across the land.

5.00–6.00   Read some chapters from the book you have chosen from the list in Appendix 1.

Day Two

9.00–9.30   Read Ephesians 1.

1. Spend time praising and thanking God for Jesus and for what He has done for us by His life and death. Use some biblical ways of expressing your praise, i.e. singing, clapping, dancing, shouting, kneeling, raising hands, etc. Try expressing your praise to God in ways you haven't used before. It might be good to use a praise tape for this (see Chapter 7 and Appendix 2).

2. Select a verse and memorise it.

9.30–11.00   Bible Study 3.

11.00–11.15   Drink and rest.

11.15–11.45   Go for a walk. As you walk thank God for the beauty you see (i.e. trees, sky, sun).

11.45–12.30   Read some chapters from the book you have chosen from the list in Appendix 1.

12.30–1.30   Drink and rest.

1.30–2.30

1. Go through the self check list on page 124 and tick each wrong attitude you see in yourself. Spend time repenting of each one and ask God to give you strength to turn away from these sins. Ask God to fill you with His Holy Spirit and give you a revival heart.

2. Are you living at peace with everyone

119

so far as it depends on you (Romans 12:8)? If not, then ask for God to forgive you and heal the circumstances/ friendships. Write a letter, make a phone call, but put the matter right.

3. Examine yourself. See if there is anything hindering your walk with Jesus. If so, ask for His wisdom— then sort it out.

2.30–3.00 Go for a walk. As you walk memorise Philippians 3:13–14.

3.00–3.15 Drink and rest.

3.15–3.45 Spend time praying for Christian organisations that work with the poor, needy, unmarried mothers, abused children, etc. (i.e. Tear Fund, Care Trust, etc.). Ask God if He would like you to be involved with any of these organisations and if so, how. (See Appendix 3 for information on various organisations.)

3.45–5.30 Read some chapters from the book you have chosen from the list in Appendix 1.

5.30–6.00 Go through all your notes. Write down what you have learned over the last two days. Have the aims been completed? Thank God for all He has begun and is going to do in you.

Bible Study 1
Nehemiah 1 and 2

Read both chapters three times.
1. Who wrote the book of Nehemiah?
2. When was it written?

3. Why was Nehemiah (a Jew) living in the citadel of Susa?
4. What was his job?
5. Did the King trust him?
6. Nehemiah had a burden for his nation. Do you have a burden for your nation? Spend five minutes asking God to give you an increasing burden for your nation.
7. His brother, Hanani, brings him bad news about the state of his nation. What is his response?
8. Have you ever wept/fasted/prayed over your nation?
9. Nehemiah became the answer to his own prayers. Are you prepared to let God use you to influence and change your nation? If so, spend a few minutes telling God you would be prepared to do anything He told you to do.
10. Write down a list of things that Nehemiah left in order to go to Jerusalem, i.e. comfort, good job, etc.
11. Go through the above list. Would you be prepared to leave these things for God?
12. Read chapter 1, verses 5 to 11. This is Nehemiah's prayer to God. Nehemiah repents before God for his nation's sins. Write down the wrong things you can see in your nation, i.e. violence, abortion, etc. Take each one individually and repent of them before God on behalf of the nation.
13. Ask God how He sees your nation. Write down His reply.
14. Before Nehemiah starts any work or tells anyone what God has told him to do, what does he do? What can we learn from this?
15. What do the enemies of the Jews say and do? (See chapter 2, verses 10 and 19.)
16. What can you learn from Nehemiah's reply to Sanballat and Tobiah? (See verse 20.)

Bible Study 2
Nehemiah 3 and 4

Read both chapters three times.

1. Each person/family had their own particular work to do. Each one was important. In God's kingdom you are important. What job has God called you to do? Are you working at it with all your might? Do you feel what you are doing is important? And why?

2. Read chapter 4, verses 1 to 6 again. Nehemiah and the Jews again receive opposition. How does Nehemiah deal with it?

3. We will always have opposition when we do something for God. How do you deal with opposition, criticism, etc.? (Answer honestly!) How should you deal with it?

4. How important is prayer to Nehemiah? Is your first thought in a crisis to pray to God?

5. Nehemiah received discouragement from his enemies (4:11), the people he was working with (4:10) and his fellow Jews (4:12). How does Nehemiah deal with it?

6. Our discouragement can come from Christians and non-Christians alike. Ask God to help you deal with discouragement in the right way. Write down things people have said or done or circumstances that have discouraged you. Go through each one and speak out the truth that God is bigger and greater than your problem.

7. It's important to notice that Nehemiah asked people to equip themselves with swords. What are our spiritual weapons? Think of ways that we can use them.

8. What is our spiritual armour? (See Ephesians 6: 10–18). Imagine yourself putting each part of

your armour on. Thank God for His armour and weapons. Take time to do this each day.

Bible Study 3
Nehemiah 5 and 6

Read both chapters three times.

1. Read chapter 5, verses 1 to 13 again. Nehemiah had a heart for the poor. Spend five minutes praying for the poor in the following situations:
   a) in Third World countries (Bangladesh, Ethiopia etc.)
   b) in your nation (homeless, etc.)
   c) in your area (terminally ill in hospital, the elderly, homeless, etc.)
   Ask God if there's any way you can help them. Write down His reply and make sure you carry it out as soon as possible.
2. Read verses 14 to 19 again. What did Nehemiah personally give to help the people/project succeed?
3. Do you tithe your income, pocket money, allowance, etc.? If not, why not?
4. What does God have to say about tithing in the Bible? (See Malachi 3:6–12.) Spend a few minutes in prayer asking God if He's pleased with the way you handle your money. Ask Him if there are any changes He'd like you to make.
5. Read chapter 6. What further things did Sanballat and Tobiah do to try and frustrate the work that Nehemiah was doing? Write down each thing.
6. How does Nehemiah deal with these attacks?
7. What happened to their enemies when the task was completed? (See 6:16.)
8. Spend some time praying for revival:

1. in yourself
2. in the church
3. in your nation.

Self Check List

1. Pride
2. Envy
3. Jealousy
4. Bitterness
5. Bad temper
6. Selfishness
7. Insensitivity
8. Unbelief
9. Ingratitude
10. Slander (i.e. speaking behind someone's back about their faults, etc.)
11. Lying (any kind of deception, i.e. hiding the full truth —perhaps only speaking half-truths)
12. Lack of love or respect for God
13. Wrong attitudes (particularly relating to prayer/Bible reading/church duties, etc.)
14. Lack of love for non-Christians
15. Worldly-mindedness (i.e. loving possessions and money more than God—acting as though you have a 'right' to them)
16. Robbing God (e.g. money, time, etc.)
17. Greed
18. Hypocrisy
19. Lust of the flesh
20. Negative or critical attitudes
21. Hardness of heart

Mini Programme 9

Day One

15 minutes	Write down any specific aims you may have in spending this time with God and ask God to begin to fulfil them in you over the next two days.
15 minutes	Read Psalm 108. Pick out one verse and meditate on it. Write down what God says to you and spend time praying thereafter.
30 minutes	Answer the following questions:

1. What is the main priority in your life?
2. What are your aims in life?
3. What are you doing practically to fulfil these aims?
4. Write down the structure of your normal working day (24-hour structure).
5. Write down the structure of a normal day off.
6. How long do you normally spend in prayer each day?
7. How long do you normally spend in Bible study?
8. How often and how long do you watch television?
9. How long do you spend physically exercising?
10. How much time do you spend in church or at church meetings?
11. How much time do you spend per week in evangelism?

30 minutes	Go for a walk. As you walk pray for your nation. Pray for your nation's leader, the

	government, the opposition parties, people in charge of the media (TV, newspapers etc.), people in charge of education. Pray for righteousness and justice.
30 minutes	Ask God how He feels about your nation. Allow Him to show you pictures/visions or lead you to Scriptures which reveal His heart. Ask Him to show you how much He loves your nation and to show you the compassion He has for the people of your land. Write down how He feels.
90 minutes	Bible Study 1.
30 minutes	Go through your answers to the questions above. Assess whether you are spending your time profitably for God's Kingdom. Are you spending too much time on television, video, etc. and not enough time in prayer? Are you fulfilling the aims you have for your life? Think of ways you can improve your lifestyle. Pray and ask God if there is anything He would like you to change. Write down what God says and if there are any changes then make sure you carry them out.

Day Two

30 minutes	Read Ephesians 1.
	1. Spend time praising and thanking God for Jesus and for what He has done for us by His life and death. Use some biblical ways of expressing your praise, i.e. singing, dancing, raising hands,

clapping, jumping, shouting, etc. Try expressing your praise to God in ways you haven't used before. It might be good to use a praise tape for this (see Chapter 7 and Appendix 2).

2. Select a verse and memorise it.

30 minutes

1. Go through the self check list on page 124 and tick each wrong attitude you see in yourself. Spend time repenting of each one and ask God to give you strength to turn away from these sins. Ask God to fill you with His Holy Spirit and give you a revival heart.

2. Are you living at peace with everyone so far as it depends on you (Romans 12:8)? If not, then ask for God to forgive you and heal the circumstances/ friendships. Write a letter, make a phone call, but put the matter right.

3. Examine yourself. See if there is anything hindering your walk with Jesus. If so, then ask for His wisdom— then sort it out.

30 minutes

Go for a walk. As you walk thank God for the beauty you see around (i.e. trees, sky, sun).

30 minutes

Spend some time praying for Christian organisations that work with the poor, needy, unmarried mothers, abused children, etc. (i.e. Tear Fund, Care Trust, etc.). Ask God if He would like you to be involved with any of these organisations and if so, how. (See Appendix 3 for information on various organisations.)

127

90 minutes   Bible Study 2.

30 minutes   Go through all your notes. Write down what you have learned over the last two days. Have the aims been completed? Thank God for all He has begun and is going to do in you.

Programme 10

Day One

9.00–9.15   Write down any specific aims you may have in spending this time with God and ask God to begin to fulfil them in you over the next two days.

9.15–9.45   Read Psalm 23. Write down what God says to you through this Psalm and spend time in prayer and praise thereafter.

9.45–11.15   Bible Study 1.

11.15–11.30   Drink and rest.

11.30–12.00   Go for a walk. Reflect on something of God's creation. Write down the thoughts God gives you.

12.00–12.30   Read 1 John 4:7–21. Answer the following questions:

1. Do you have fear in your heart—if so, why? Write down the things that you are fearful about.
2. How do you get rid of fear?
3. Do you have anger in your heart—if so, why? Write down some of the things you are angry about.
4. How do you get rid of anger?
5. Spend time praying and asking God to take away any fear and/or anger you may have.

12.30–1.30   Drink and rest.

1.30–2.00   Read 2 Timothy 1:7. Spend five minutes meditating on this verse. Write down what you get. Write down the giftings you believe God has given you (natural

129

	giftings as well as spiritual giftings). Spend time asking God for opportunities to share your giftings with others.
2.00–3.30	Bible Study 2.
3.30–3.45	Drink and rest.
3.45–4.30	Write down all the good things God has done in your life and thank Him for them. Spend time praising God for all He's done for you. Use some biblical ways of expressing your praise, i.e. singing, clapping, dancing, shouting, kneeling, raising of hands, etc. Try expressing your praise to God in ways you haven't used before. It might be good to use a praise tape for this (see Chapter 7 and Appendix 2).
4.30–5.00	Spend this time with your pastor/leader/counsellor if appropriate or spend time praying about the areas God highlighted today.

Day Two

9.00–9.30	Read Psalm 8. Write down what God says to you through this Psalm and spend time in prayer and praise thereafter.
9.30–11.00	Bible Study 3.
11.00–11.15	Drink and rest.
11.15–11.45	Go for a walk. Ask God how He feels about you and what He thinks of you. Write down His reply.
11.45–12.30	Read 1 Corinthians 13.
	1. Look up the meaning of the word 'love' in the dictionary. Write it down.

2. Write down what love means to you.
3. Write down what love is, according to this chapter.
4. Write down what love *isn't*, according to this chapter.
5. Look up and write out the following verses which all talk of love:

   • Deuteronomy 6:5 • Leviticus 19:18
   • Proverbs 17:17   • Matthew 5:44
   • Ephesians 5:1–2 • John 13:35
   • John 15:13   • Romans 12:9
   • Galatians 5:13   • 1 John 4:7–8

12.30–1.30   Drink and rest.

1.30–2.00   Read 1 Kings 19:1–8. Answer the following questions:
1. Verse 3 says Elijah was afraid. Why was he afraid?
2. In verse 4 Elijah gets so depressed he prays that he might die. What is the reason for this? See chapter 18.
3. How does God deal with Elijah?
4. Would you expect God to treat you the same way?

2.00–3.00   Meditate on 1 John 4:18.
1. Write down what God says to you through your meditation.
2. Pray (or ask someone to pray for you) and ask God to take away any fear in your life and replace it with a deep knowledge of His love.
3. Ask God how much He loves you. Write down His reply.

131

4. Read Ephesians 3:16–21. This is Paul's prayer for the Ephesians. Write down what God says to you through these verses. Also, make his prayer yours—pray this prayer out loud to God making it personal to you, (i.e. 'I pray that out of His glorious riches He will strengthen me with power through His Spirit in my inner being' etc.)

3.00–3.15 Drink and rest.

3.15–3.30 Spend time worshipping God. Use some biblical ways of expressing your worship i.e. singing, raising hands, speaking, kneeling, bowing, lying prostrate, etc. Try expressing your worship in ways you haven't used before. It might be good to use a worship tape for this (see Chapter 7 and Appendix 2). Thank Him for all He's doing in you during this time of seeking Him.

3.30–4.15 Ask God if there is anything specific He wants you to do with your life. Write down His reply.

4.15–5.00 Spend this time with your pastor/leader/counsellor if appropriate, or look again at the aims of this time with God and spend time thanking Him for all He's begun to do in you during the last two days.

Bible Study 1
Hebrews 11

Read the chapter at least three times.
1. Who wrote the book of Hebrews?
2. When was it written?

3. To whom was it written?
4. What was the reason for writing?
5a. What is faith?
  b. How many times is 'faith' mentioned in this chapter?
  c. How important is faith to God? Find a verse in Scripture to back up your answer.
6. Read Genesis 4:1–16. Write down what you can learn through this story.
7. Read verse 4. What does it mean that Abel still speaks today?
8. Where else in Scripture is Enoch mentioned?
9. Meditate on verse 6. Write down what God says to you through your meditation.
10. Verse 7 mentions that Noah built the ark in 'holy fear'. What is the difference between fear and holy fear?
11. Paraphrase verse 11.

Bible Study 2
Hebrews 11

Read the chapter again.
1. Paraphrase verse 13.
2. Verse 16 says they were longing for a better country— a heavenly one. Do you long for heaven and to be with Jesus? Do you often think of the future? If not, why not? Do you have any fear of death or fear of the future? Spend time praying that God may give you a deeper desire for Him and take away any fears you may have.
3. Read verses 17 to 19. Read Genesis 22:1–19. How would you react if God asked you to 'sacrifice' something or someone dear to you? Spend a few minutes asking God to give you right motives and attitudes.

4. Read verse 24. Can you think of someone else in the Bible who chose to do right and consequently suffered rather than 'enjoy the pleasures of sin for a short time'?

5. How do you react to suffering? Write down your reactions.

6. How did Jesus react to suffering? Write down His reactions.

7. Write down some verses in Scripture that would tell us how we should react to suffering/persecution.

8. Spend some time praying and asking God to take away the fear of suffering/persecution and ask Him to help you react the way Jesus did.

Bible Study 3
Hebrews 11

Read the chapter again.

1. Verse 27. Moses kept his spiritual eyes open and 'saw him who is invisible'. Often we take our eyes off Jesus and put them on our circumstances. How should we practically react through difficult circumstances?

2. Read 2 Kings 6:8–18. Write down what God says to you through these verses.

3. Write down the things that Jesus has done for you on the cross. Thank Him for each one.

4. Read verse 31. Rahab was a prostitute, yet God saved her when the walls of Jericho fell. Why? What does this tell you about God?

5. Is faith on its own good enough? See James 2:14. Give reasons for your answer.

6. Verse 39. There are many persons named in this chapter who did not see the promises of God fulfilled

in their lifetime. However, even when they were
dying, they still had faith that God would accomplish
all that He had said. Write down what God has
promised you. Do you believe that He can bring it into
being?

7. Spend time thanking God for all the promises He has
given you and ask Him to increase your faith in Him.

8. Write down the main things God has said to you
through this chapter.

Mini Programme 10

Day One

15 minutes	Write down any specific aims you may have in spending this time with God and ask Him to begin to fulfil them in you over the next two days.
30 minutes	Read Psalm 23. Write down what God says to you through this Psalm and spend time in prayer and praise thereafter.
15 minutes	Go for a walk. Reflect on something of God's creation. Write down the thoughts God gives you.
30 minutes	Read 1 John 4:7–21. Answer the following questions:

1. Do you have fear in your heart—if so, why? Write down the things that you are fearful about.
2. How do you get rid of fear?
3. Do you have anger in your heart—if so, why? Write down some of the things you are angry about.
4. How do you get rid of anger?
5. Spend time praying and asking God to take away any fear and/or anger you may have.

90 minutes	Bible Study 1.
30 minutes	Read 2 Timothy 1:7. Spend five minutes meditating on this verse. Write down what you get. Write down the giftings you believe God has given you (natural giftings as well as spiritual giftings). Spend time asking God for opportunities to share

your giftings with others.

30 minutes Write down all the good things God has done in your life and thank Him for them. Spend time praising God for all He's done for you. Use some biblical ways of expressing your praise, i.e. singing, clapping, dancing, shouting, kneeling, raising of hands, etc. Try expressing your praise to God in ways you haven't used before. It might be good to use a praise tape for this (see Chapter 7 and Appendix 2).

Day Two

30 minutes Read Psalm 8. Write down what God says to you through this Psalm and spend time in prayer and praise thereafter.

30 minutes Read 1 Kings 19:1–8. Answer the following questions:
1. Verse 3 says Elijah was afraid. Why was he afraid?
2. In verse 4 Elijah gets so down and depressed he prays that he might die. What is the reason for this? See chapter 18.
3. How does God deal with Elijah?
4. Would you expect God to treat you the same way?

15 minutes Go for a walk. Ask God how He feels about you and what He thinks of you. Write down His reply.

45 minutes Read 1 Corinthians 13.
1. Look up the meaning of the word 'love'

in the dictionary. Write it down.

2. Write down what love means to you.
3. Write down what love is, according to this chapter.
4. Write down what love *isn't,* according to this chapter.
5. Look up and write out in full the following verses which all talk of love.

- Deuteronomy 6:5
- Proverbs 17:17
- Ephesians 5:1–2
- John 15:13
- Galatians 5:13
- Leviticus 19:18
- Matthew 5:44
- John 13:35
- Romans 12:9
- 1 John 4:7–8.

90 minutes   Bible Study 2.

15 minutes   Spend time worshipping God. Use some biblical ways of expressing your worship, i.e. singing, raising hands, speaking, kneeling, bowing, lying prostrate, etc. Try expressing your worship in ways you haven't used before. It might be good to use a worship tape for this (see Chapter 7 and Appendix 2). Thank Him for all He's doing in you during this time of seeking Him.

15 minutes   Spend this time with your pastor/leader/ counsellor if appropriate, or look again at the aims of this time with God and spend time thanking Him for all He's begun to do in you during the last two days.

Programme 11

Day One

9.00–9.15	Write down any specific aims you may have in spending this time with God and ask Him to begin to fulfil them in you over the next two days.
9.15–9.45	Read Psalm 27. Write down what God says to you through this chapter and spend time praying thereafter.
9.45–11.15	Bible Study 1.
11.15–11.30	Drink and rest.
11.30–12.00	Go for a walk. Meditate on something of God's creation. Write down the thoughts God gives you.
12.00–12.30	Read some chapters from the book you have chosen from the list in Appendix 1.
12.30–1.30	Drink and rest.
1.30–2.15	Read 1 Corinthians 13.

1. Write out verses 4–8 finishing with the phrase 'love never fails'. It says in Scripture 'God is love'. Read the passage again replacing the word 'love' with 'God'. Spend a few minutes thanking God for who He is and how He treats you.

2. Think of your love towards God first of all, then think of your love towards others (family, friends, etc.). How does your love compare to God's? Spend a few minutes repenting of the times you

	have failed and ask God to give you a deeper love for Him and for others.
2.15–2.30	Drink and rest.
2.30–4.00	Bible Study 2.
4.00–4.30	Write down all the good things God has done in your life and thank Him for them. Spend time praising God for all He's done for you. Use some biblical ways of expressing your praise, i.e. singing, clapping, dancing, shouting, kneeling, raising hands, etc. Try expressing your praise to God in ways you haven't used before. It might be good to use a praise tape for this (see Chapter 7 and Appendix 2).
4.30–5.30	Read some chapters from the book you have chosen from the list in Appendix 1.
5.30–6.00	Spend this time with your pastor/leader/counsellor if appropriate or spend time praying about all God has done in you today.

Day Two

9.00–9.30	Read Psalm 34. Write down what God says to you through this chapter and spend time praying thereafter.
9.30–11.00	Bible Study 3.
11.00–11.15	Drink and rest.
11.15–11.45	Go for a walk. Ask God how He feels about you and what He thinks of you. Write down His reply.

11.45–12.30 Read some chapters from the book you have chosen from the list in Appendix 1.

12.30–1.30 Drink and rest.

1.30–2.00 Write down anything you want God to do in you and anything you want released from. Pray about each thing.

2.00–2.30 Read 1 John 4:7—5:3. Write down what you get from these verses.

2.30–2.45 Drink and rest.

2.45–3.15 Answer the following questions:
1. Do you find it easy/hard to trust God? Why?
2. Are you willing to let Him have His way in your life no matter what it costs? If the answer is no, then write down the reasons why.
3. Is there anything in your life that would stop/hinder you following God? If yes, write down what it is.
4. Have you put God as boss/Number One in your life?
5. Spend a few minutes praying about your answers.

3.15–3.45 Write a letter to God. Read it out loud to Him. Spend time praising God, using some biblical ways of expressing your praise, i.e. singing, clapping, dancing, shouting, kneeling, raising hands, etc. Try expressing your praise to God in ways you haven't used before. It might be good to use a praise tape for this (see Chapter 7 and Appendix 2).

3.45–5.30   Read some chapters from the book you have chosen from the list in Appendix 1.

5.30–6.00   Spend this time with your leader/pastor/counsellor if appropriate or look again at the aims of this time with God. Write down what you feel God has done or has started to do in you during these two days. Thank Him for what He's done.

Bible Study 1
Romans 8

Read the chapter at least three times.
Read verses 1 to 17.

1. Who wrote Romans?
2. When was it written?
3. Where was it written?
4. To whom was it written?
5. Why was it written?
6. Read verse 1. Write down the kinds of things that Satan uses to condemn you.
7. Memorise verse 1.
8. Why is there now no condemnation for us?
9. Read verse 5. Have you got your mind set on what the Spirit desires? How should we live according to these verses?
10. What happens spiritually if you live according to the sinful nature?
11. What is the main thing God has said to you through these verses?

Bible Study 2
Romans 8

Read the chapter again.
Read verses 18 to 27.

1. Write down any sufferings you may be going through at this present time.
2. What kind of suffering did Jesus go through during His time on earth? How did He react to suffering? Find a verse in Scripture to back up your answer.
3. Meditate on verse 18. Write down what you get.
4. Memorise verse 18.
5. Read verse 22. Why is creation groaning?
6. Read verse 24. What is our hope?
7. Read verses 26 and 27. How does the Holy Spirit help us in our prayers?
8. Paraphrase verses 26 and 27.
9. Pray for each suffering you are going through. Ask God to give you patience and wisdom to endure to the end.
10. What is the main thing God has said to you through these verses?

Bible Study 3
Romans 8

Read the chapter again.
Read verses 28 to 39.

1. Memorise verse 28.
2. Ask God to speak to you through verse 28. Write down what He says.

3. Meditate on verse 31. Write down what God says.
4. Paraphrase verses 31 to 34.
5. Verse 34 tells us that Jesus is interceding for us at the right hand of God. Think about that for a couple of minutes. Write down how that makes you feel.
6. Write out verses 37 to 39 in full. Ask God to speak to you through these verses. Write down what He says.
7. Ask God how big His love is for you. Write down His reply.
8. Find a verse in Scripture that tells you how big His love is for you.
9. What is the main thing God has said to you through these verses?

REMEMBER

> *Write down all that God says to you.*

Mini Programme 11

Day One

15 minutes   Write down any specific aims you may have in spending this time with God and ask Him to begin to fulfil them in you over the next two days.

30 minutes   Read Psalm 27. Write down what God says to you through this chapter and spend time praying thereafter.

15 minutes   Go for a walk. Meditate on something of God's creation. Write down the thoughts God gives you.

45 minutes   Read 1 Corinthians 13.

1. Write out verses 4 to 8 finishing with the phrase 'love never fails'. It says in Scripture 'God is love'. Read the passage again replacing the word 'love' with 'God'. Spend a few minutes thanking God for who He is and how He treats you.

2. Think of your love towards God first of all, then think of your love towards others (family, friends, etc.). How does your love compare to God's? Spend a few minutes repenting of the times you have failed and ask God to give you a deeper love for Him and for others.

90 minutes   Bible Study 1.

30 minutes   Write down all the good things God has done in your life and thank Him for them. Spend some time praising God for all He's done for you. Use some biblical ways of

expressing your praise, i.e. singing, clapping, dancing, shouting, kneeling, raising hands, etc. Try expressing your praise to God in ways you haven't used before. It might be good to use a praise tape for this (see Chapter 7 and Appendix 2).

15 minutes   Spend this time with your pastor/leader/ counsellor if appropriate or spend time praying about all God has done in you today.

Day Two

30 minutes   Read Psalm 34. Write down what God says to you through this chapter and spend time praying thereafter.

30 minutes   Go for a walk. Ask God how He feels about you and what He thinks of you. Write down His reply.

30 minutes   Read 1 John 4:7—5:3. Write down what you get from these verses.

30 minutes   Answer the following questions:

1. Do you find it easy/hard to trust God? Why?
2. Are you willing to let Him have His way in your life no matter what it costs? If the answer is no, then write down the reasons why.
3. Is there anything in your life that would stop/hinder you following God? If yes, write down what it is.
4. Have you put God as boss/Number One in your life?

146

5. Spend a few minutes praying about your answers.

90 minutes   Bible Study 2.

30 minutes   Spend this time with your leader/pastor/counsellor if appropriate, or look again at the aims of this time with God. Write down what you feel God has done or has started to do in you during these two days. Thank Him for what He's done.

Programme 12

Day One

9.00–9.15   Write down any specific aims you may
            have in spending this time with God and
            ask Him to begin to fulfil them in you over
            the next few days.

9.15–9.45   Read Psalm 19. Write down what God says
            to you through this Psalm and spend time in
            prayer and praise thereafter.

9.45–11.15 Bible Study 1.

11.15–11.30 Drink and rest.

11.30–12.00 Go for a walk. Reflect on something of
            God's creation (i.e. trees, flowers etc.).
            Write down the thoughts God gives you.

12.00–12.30 Read 1 John 4:7–21. Answer the following
            questions:

1. Do you have fear in your heart? If so,
   why? How do we get rid of fear?

2. Do you have anger in your heart? If so,
   why? How do we get rid of anger?

3. Read verse 20. How should you treat
   someone you don't naturally get on
   with? Do you find this easy/hard?
   Why?

4. Meditate on verse 13. Write down
   what God gives you.

5. What are the main things God says to
   you through these verses?

12.30–1.30 Drink and rest.

1.30–2.00   Write down the names of two people you
            find it difficult to get on with. Pray for them
            and ask God to give you something for

148

them to encourage them. Give whatever you get to them at some point in the next three days to encourage them. (If they are not nearby then write it down and send it to them.)

2.00–3.30	Bible Study 2.
3.30–3.45	Drink and rest.
3.45–4.45	Write down all the good things God has done in your life and thank Him for them. Spend time praising God for all He's done for you. Use some biblical ways of expressing your praise, i.e. singing, clapping, dancing, shouting, kneeling, raising hands, etc. Try expressing your praise to God in ways you haven't used before. It might be good to use a praise tape for this (see Chapter 7 and Appendix 2).
4.45–5.30	Read some chapters from the book you have chosen from the list in Appendix 1.
5.30–6.00	Spend time praying with leader/ counsellor/pastor if appropriate or spend time praying about all God has done in you today.

Day Two

9.00–9.30	Read 1 Peter 4 twice. Write down what God says to you through this chapter. Spend at least ten minutes praying about the things you have heard from God.
9.30–11.00	Bible Study 3.
11.00–11.15	Drink and rest.
11.15–11.45	Go for a walk. Ask God how He feels about

	you and what He thinks of you. Write down His reply.
11.45–12.30	Read some chapters from the book you have chosen from the list in Appendix 1.
12.30–1.30	Drink and rest.
1.30–2.00	Read 1 Corinthians 13 twice.

1. Write down all the things that love is.
2. Write down all the things love isn't.
3. Write down what God says to you through this chapter.
4. Ask for more of God's love to be shown through you.

2.00–2.45	Answer the following questions:

1. Write down your giftings as you see them (natural giftings as well as spiritual). Thank God for what He has done and what He is doing.
2. Write down your failings. Pray about each one. Ask God to give you something to counteract each one. Write down what God gives you.
3. Go through the self check list on page 156. Tick off each thing you find in yourself. Then ask God for forgiveness for each one.
4. Ask God to remind you of anything you have done in the past that is wrong and for which you need His forgiveness. (Please don't bring up sins for which God has already forgiven you.) Write them down on a piece of paper and ask God to forgive you for each thing. Then tear it up and put it in a rubbish bin.

	Spend time thanking God for His forgiveness.
2.45–3.00	Drink and rest.
3.00–3.30	Spend time praising God for all He's done for you. Use some biblical ways of expressing your praise, i.e. singing, clapping, dancing, shouting, kneeling, raising hands, etc. Try expressing your praise to God in ways you haven't used before. It might be good to use a praise tape for this (see Chapter 7 and Appendix 2).
3.30–5.00	Read some chapters from the book you have chosen from the list in Appendix 1.

Day Three

9.00–9.45	Read the book of James. Write down anything God says to you through the reading of this book. Spend time praying thereafter.
9.45–11.15	Bible Study 4.
11.15–11.30	Drink and rest.
11.30–12.00	Go for a walk. Pray for your family and friends as you walk.
12.00–12.30	Answer the following questions:
	1. How long do you normally pray for?
	2. How hard do you find prayer?
	3. How could you improve your quiet time?
	4. Spend time praying about the above answers.
12.30–1.30	Drink and rest.
1.30–2.30	Write down the name of someone who you

151

know has been abused (sexually, physically or emotionally). Pray for them for ten minutes. Ask God to give you a heart for them and for people like them who have been abused. Ask God also to give you a heart for the poor and needy. Ask God what needs to change in you to be able to have more of a heart for those who are hurting. Write down what He says.

2.30–3.00   Read Matthew 25:31–46. Write down what God says to you through these verses.

3.00–3.15   Drink and rest.

3.15–5.00   Read some chapters from the book you have chosen from the list in Appendix 1.

5.00–6.00   Read again the aims of your time with God. Has He begun to do the things you have asked Him to do? Spend time praying on your own, or if appropriate with your leader/pastor/counsellor, about all the things you have learned through the last few days.

Bible Study 1
John 13

Read the chapter at least three times.
1. Who wrote the book of John?
2. When was it written?
3. Where was it written?
4. To whom was it written?
5. How many times in verses 1 to 17 does John say 'Jesus knew'?
6. Look at each instance and write down how Jesus knew. Can we have the same insight into things and circumstances as Jesus did?

7. Why did Jesus wash His disciples' feet?
8. Imagine Jesus washing your feet. How do you feel? Write down your thoughts.
9. Read verses 14 and 15. What can we do to follow Jesus' example and obey him by 'washing other people's feet'?
10. Read verse 21. Jesus knew that one of His disciples was going to betray Him. Write down the emotions Jesus must have been feeling at this time.
11. Read verses 34 and 35. Find a verse in Scripture that shows you how much Jesus loves us.
12. How easy/hard do you find it to express your love to others? And why?
13. What verse(s) speak(s) to you most and why?

Bible Study 2
John 14

Read the chapter at least three times.
1. In verse 1, why were the disciples' hearts troubled?
2. Write down what kinds of things trouble your heart. Spend some time asking God for His peace in your life.
3. In verse 1 Jesus says not to be troubled, but to TRUST in God and in Him! What does it mean to TRUST?
4. How easy/hard do you find trusting God? And why?
5. How easy/hard do you find trusting others? And why?
6. Paraphrase verses 12 to 14.
7. Memorise verse 14.
8. How does God know if we love Him? See verses 15, 21 and 23.
9. Who is the Counsellor mentioned in verse 16?

10. How well do you know the Counsellor and have you given Him access to your life?
11. Meditate on verse 27. Write down what you get.
12. Who is the 'prince of this world' mentioned in verse 30?
13. What verse(s) speak(s) to you the most and why?

Bible Study 3
John 15

Read the chapter at least three times.
1. Paraphrase verses 1 to 4.
2. Meditate on verse 4. Write down what God says to you.
3. What does it mean when Jesus says that God 'prunes' us?
4. Have you experienced that happening in your life? Give examples.
5. Memorise verse 7.
6. Write down in a couple of sentences what Jesus is trying to communicate to us in this chapter.
7. Meditate on verses 14 and 15. Write down what God says to you through your meditation.
8. Verses 14 and 15 say that Jesus regards us as His friends. Spend a few minutes thanking Jesus for His friendship and telling Him how much it means to you.
9. Verses 16 and 19 say that Jesus chose us. Find another verse in Scripture to back this up.
10. Write down what 'chosen' means (it may help to use a dictionary). Meditate on the fact that Jesus has chosen you for Himself. How does it make you feel?
11. What verses have spoken to you the most and why?
12. Write down the main things you received from the Lord during this Bible study.

Bible Study 4
James 2

Read the chapter at least three times.
1. Who wrote James?
2. When was it written?
3. Where was it written?
4. To whom was it written?
5. Look up the word 'favouritism'. Write down its meaning. This chapter is about favouring the rich over the poor. In what other ways can we sin by showing favouritism? How can we avoid this?
6. Read verse 8. The royal law is to 'love your neighbour as yourself'. Do you find it easy/hard to love and accept yourself? Give reasons.
7. The royal law leaves no room for selfishness. Spend some time asking God to reveal times when you haven't loved your neighbour as yourself. Ask God to help you be more aware of selfishness in your life and to help you put it to death.
8. Paraphrase verses 12 and 13.
9. Read verse 14. What does this verse mean?
10. How is our faith made complete according to verse 22? What does this mean practically?
11. Read verses 20 to 26. Write down what God says to you from these verses!
12. Write down the main things God has said to you through this chapter.

REMEMBER

> *Warm-up and wind-down are very important in physical exercise. Make sure you look at the pre- and postexercise instructions in Chapter 2.*

Self Check List

1. Pride
2. Envy
3. Jealousy
4. Bitterness
5. Bad temper
6. Selfishness
7. Insensitivity
8. Unbelief
9. Ingratitude
10. Slander (i.e. speaking behind someone's back about their faults, etc.)
11. Lying (any kind of deception, i.e. hiding the full truth —perhaps only speaking half-truths)
12. Lack of love or respect for God
13. Wrong attitudes (particularly relating to prayer/ Bible reading/church duties, etc.)
14. Lack of love for non-Christians
15. Worldly-mindedness (i.e. loving possessions and money more than God—acting as though you have a 'right' to them)
16. Robbing God (e.g. money, time, etc.)
17. Greed
18. Hypocrisy
19. Lust of the flesh
20. Negative or critical attitudes
21. Hardness of heart

Mini Programme 12

Day One

15 minutes	Write down any specific aims you may have in spending this time with God and ask Him to begin to fulfil them in you over the next few days.
30 minutes	Read Psalm 19. Write down what God says to you through this Psalm and spend time in prayer and praise thereafter.
15 minutes	Go for a walk. Reflect on something of God's creation (i.e. trees, flowers, etc.). Write down the thoughts God gives you.
30 minutes	Read 1 John 4:7–21. Answer the following questions:

1. Do you have fear in your heart? If so, why? How do we get rid of fear?
2. Do you have anger in your heart? If so, why? How do we get rid of anger?
3. Read verse 20. How should you treat someone you don't naturally get on with? Do you find this easy/hard? Why?
4. Meditate on verse 13. Write down what God gives you.
5. What are the main things God says to you through these verses?

90 minutes	Bible Study 1.
30 minutes	Write down the names of two people you find it difficult to get on with. Pray for them and ask God to give you something for them to encourage them. Give whatever you get to them at some point in the next

	three days to encourage them. (If they are not nearby then write it down and send it to them.)
30 minutes	Write down all the good things God has done in your life and thank Him for them. Spend time praising God for all He's done for you. Use some biblical ways of expressing your praise, i.e. singing, clapping, dancing, shouting, kneeling, raising hands, etc. Try expressing your praise to God in ways you haven't used before. It might be good to use a praise tape for this (see Chapter 7 and Appendix 2).

Day Two

30 minutes	Read 1 Peter 4 twice. Write down what God says to you through this chapter. Spend at least ten minutes praying about the things you have heard from God.
30 minutes	Go for a walk. Ask God how He feels about you and what He thinks of you. Write down His reply.
45 minutes	Answer the following questions:

1. Write down your giftings as you see them (natural giftings as well as spiritual). Thank God for what He has done and what He is doing.
2. Write down your failings. Pray about each one. Ask God to give you something to counteract each one.

Write down what God gives you.

3. Go through the self check list on page 156. Tick off each thing you find in yourself. Then ask God for forgiveness for each one.

4. Ask God to remind you of anything that you have done in the past that is wrong and for which you need His forgiveness. (Please don't bring up sins for which God has already forgiven you.) Write it down on a piece of paper and ask God to forgive you for each thing. Then tear it up and put it in a rubbish bin. Spend time thanking God for His forgiveness.

15 minutes   Spend time praising God for all He's done for you. Use some biblical ways of expressing your praise, i.e. singing, clapping, dancing, shouting, kneeling, raising hands, etc. Try expressing your praise to God in ways you haven't used before. It might be good to use a praise tape for this (see Chapter 7 and Appendix 2).

90 minutes   Bible Study 2.

30 minutes   Read 1 Corinthians 13 twice.

1. Write down all the things that love is.

2. Write down all the things love isn't.

3. Write down what God says to you through this chapter.

4. Ask for more of God's love to be shown through you.

159

Day Three

45 minutes	Read the book of James. Write down anything God says to you through the reading of this book. Spend time praying thereafter.
15 minutes	Go for a walk. Pray for your family and friends as you walk.
60 minutes	Write down the name of someone who you know has been abused (sexually, physically or emotionally). Pray for them for ten minutes. Ask God to give you a heart for them and for people like them who have been abused. Ask God also to give you a heart for the poor and needy. Ask God what needs to change in you to be able to have more of a heart for those who are hurting. Write down what He says.
90 minutes	Bible Study 3.
30 minutes	Read again the aims of your time with God. Has He begun to do the things you have asked Him to do? Spend time praying on your own, or if appropriate with your leader/pastor/counsellor, about all the things you have learned through the last few days.

Programme 13

Day One

9.00–9.15	Write down any specific aims you may have in spending this time with God and ask Him to begin to fulfil them over the next few days.
9.15–9.45	Read John 16:5–33. Write down what God says to you through these verses. Spend time praying thereafter.
9.45–11.15	Bible Study 1.
11.15–11.30	Drink and rest.
11.30–12.00	Go for a walk. Ask God to speak to you through nature Write down what He says. Praise Him for His love for you.
12.00–12.30	Read some chapters from the book you have chosen from the list in Appendix 1.
12.30–1.30	Drink and rest.
1.30–3.00	Bible Study 2.
3.00-3.30	Spend time praising God. Use some biblical ways of expressing your praise, i.e. singing, clapping, dancing, shouting, kneeling, raising hands, etc. Try expressing your praise to God in ways you haven't used before. It might be good to use a praise tape for this. (see Chapter 7 and Appendix 2).
3.30–3.45	Drink and rest.
3.45–4.15	Answer the following questions:

1. What is your deepest desire?
2. Do you feel secure in your friendship with God? If not, why not?

3. What kind of picture do you have of God?
4. What do you want God to do for you?
5. What do you want to do with your life? What are you aiming for?
6. What are you doing practically to outwork your answer to No. 5?

4.15–4.30   Meditate on John 16:33. Write down what God says to you.

4.30–6.00   Read some chapters from the book you have chosen from the list in Appendix 1.

Day Two

9.00–9.30   Read Isaiah 62. Write down what God says to you through this chapter. Spend time in prayer thereafter.

9.30–11.00   Bible Study 3.

11.00–11.30   Go for a walk. Ask God how He feels about you and for a picture of how much He loves you. Write down what God says.

11.30–11.45   Drink and rest.

11.45–12.30   Read Hebrews 12 twice. Write down what you get from this chapter, then answer the following questions:

1. In verse 1, who are the 'cloud of witnesses'?
2. In verse 2, how do we practically 'throw off everything that hinders and the sin that so easily entangles'?
3. Write down what things in your life would 'hinder' you or any sins that would easily 'entangle' you.

162

           4. Ask God for His forgiveness and cleansing for the above and ask the Holy Spirit to fill you anew.

           5. How do you react to discipline (verse 7)? And how should we react?

           6. Verse 14 tells us to be 'holy'. Look up the meaning of the word 'holy' in a dictionary. How do we become holy?

12.30–1.30   Drink and rest.

1.30–2.00   Make a list of all the good things God has done for you throughout your life and spend time praising Him for them. Use some biblical ways of expressing your praise, i.e. singing, clapping, dancing, shouting, kneeling, raising hands, etc. Try expressing your praise to God in ways you haven't used before. It might be good to use a praise tape (see Chapter 7 and Appendix 2).

2.00–3.30   Bible Study 4.

3.30–3.45   Drink and rest.

3.45–4.15   Go for a walk. Meditate on James 1:22 while you walk. Write down what God says to you through your meditation.

4.15–6.00   Read some chapters from the book you have chosen from the list in Appendix 1.

Day Three

9.00–9.30   Read Psalm 145. Write down all God says to you through this Psalm. Spend time praising Him for all His faithfulness.

9.30–11.00   Bible Study 5.

11.00–11.15   Go for a walk. Pray for non-Christian

	family or friends as you walk.
11.15–11.30	Drink and rest.
11.30–12.00	Answer the following questions:

1. Do you have any non-Christian friends? If not, why not and how could you develop friendships with others who are not Christians in order to help them?
2. Do you pray for any non-Christians regularly?
3. How often do you pray for the rulers of your nation?
4. Do you pray for God's influence to come in the media? in education? in politics?
5. Do you pray for the children of your land who are being abused, etc.? (You only need to pick up a newspaper to see many stories of hurt children.)
6. Spend five minutes praying about each subject above, i.e. the government, education, media, etc.

12.00–12.30	Read some chapters from the book you have chosen from the list in Appendix 1.
12.30–1.30	Drink and rest.
1.30–2.00	Read 1 Timothy 6:3–21. The downfall of many people can be the 'love of money'. How do you cope with money? Answer the following questions:

1. Do you feel that tithing is necessary?
2. Do you tithe your money faithfully each week/month?
3. Are you a generous giver?
4. Do you grudge spending money on yourself?

5. What would you do if you saw someone in need, but had already given your tithe for this month?
6. Have you ever had to 'live by faith'—in other words completely depend on God for finance? If so, what was your experience? If not, what would be your reaction if God asked you to do so?
7. Examine yourself—does everything in your life revolve around money?
8. What does Paul tell us in this chapter to pursue?
9. Is there anything wrong in being rich, according to this chapter?
10. If we are rich, how does Paul tell us to act?
11. What can you learn from this chapter, and the answers to the above questions, about yourself and money?
12. Spend a few minutes asking God if there is anything He wants to say to you about your finances. Write down anything He says and put it into practice as soon as you can.

2.00–2.30 Go for a walk. Praise God for who He is and for what He means to you as you walk.
2.30–2.45 Drink and rest.
2.45–4.30 Read some chapters from the book you have chosen from the list in Appendix 1.
4.30–5.00 Pray with your leader/counsellor/pastor if appropriate or spend time praying about all God has said to you today.

Day Four

9.00–9.30   Read Isaiah 65:17–25. Write down what God says to you through these verses.

9.30–11.00   Bible Study 6.

11.00–11.15   Drink and rest.

11.15–12.00   Go for a walk. Pray about Christ's return to earth as you walk.

12.00–12.30   Answer the following questions:

1. Do you have a fear of the future? If so, which aspects of the future worry you and why?
2. Are you afraid of death?
3. Do you often think of Christ's return?
4. Which emotion do you portray when you think of Jesus coming back again?
5. Look up Philippians 1:21. In all honesty, could you say what Paul has said here? If not, write down your reasons why.

12.30–1.30   Drink and rest.

1.30–2.00   Read 1 Thessalonians 4:13–18 and 1 Thessalonians 5:1–11. Answer the following questions:

1. 1 Thessalonians 4:18 and 5:11 say we should 'encourage each other'. After reading these verses do you feel encouraged, and why?
2. Read chapter 5, verse 6. What can we do practically to outwork this verse?
3. Meditate on chapter 5, verse 10. What does God say to you through this verse?

	4. Write down the main things God says to you through these verses.
2.00–2.45	Spend time praying about your answers to the questions in today's programme. If you need to repent of anything, then do so. If you need more of God's love, then ask God for it. Whatever you need to be more in love with Jesus and to welcome His return, then ask God for it in prayer. Then spend time worshipping God for who He is —for His plans for your life and for His plans for the world. Use some of the biblical ways to worship, i.e. singing, raising hands, speaking, kneeling, bowing, lying prostrate, etc. It might be good to use a worship tape (see Chapter 7 and Appendix 2).
2.45–3.15	Go for a walk. Meditate on and thank God for the beauty of nature around you as you walk.
3.15–3.30	Drink and rest.
3.30–5.30	Read some chapters from the book you have chosen from the list in Appendix 1.
5.30–6.00	Pray with your leader/counsellor/pastor if appropriate, or spend time praying with a friend or on your own about all God has said to you today.

Day Five

| 9.00–9.30 | Read Psalm 24. Write down all that God says to you through the Psalm. Spend a few minutes praying about what God says. |

9.30–11.00	Bible Study 7.
11.00–11.30	Go for a walk. Pray for revival for your nation as you walk. Ask God to give you a revival heart.
11.30–11.45	Drink and rest.
11.45–12.30	Read some chapters from the book you have chosen from the list in Appendix 1.
12.30–1.30	Drink and rest.
1.30–2.00	Revival always begins in the church!

1. Spend time examining yourself and your life to see if there is anything God would like to change.
2. Go through the self check list on pages 176 and 177 and see if any of these wrong attitudes are in you.
3. Spend time praying and repenting of anything God highlights.
4. Take a note of anything God tells you to do (e.g. apologise to someone; change attitude, etc.).

2.00–2.30	Meditate on Habakkuk 1:5. Write down what God says to you. Pray about what you receive from God.
2.30–3.00	Read Habakkuk 2:2–3. Answer the following questions:

1. Have you caught revival in your spirit? If not, then ask God if there's anything He'd like to tell you about revival.
2. If so, are you convinced God has said that revival is coming to your nation?
3. According to these verses, what should

          we do if years pass by, but revival has not yet come?

4. Paraphrase the two verses.
5. Ask God to speak to you through them. Write down what He says.

3.00–3.15   Drink and rest.

3.15–3.45   Ask God how He feels about the following subjects. Spend a few minutes on each. Write down what God says.

1. Your nation as a whole
2. The media
3. Crime and violence in your nation
4. The many injustices that happen
5. The poor and needy

Pray about the following subjects, spending a few minutes on each subject:

1. Violence in your nation
2. Abortions
3. Child abuse (physical and sexual)
4. Homelessness
5. The poor and needy

3.45–4.15   Go for a walk. As you walk pray for the church worldwide. Thank God for the 'New Generation' He is raising up as an army to fight the enemy. Write down anything God says to you.

4.15–5.30   Read some chapters from the book you have chosen fron the list in Appendix 1.

5.30–6.00   Pray with your leader/counsellor/pastor—or spend time looking through all your notes and thanking God for all He's done in you during the last five days.

Developing Spiritual Wholeness

Bible Study 1
Philippians 1:1–26

Read the passage at least three times.
1. Who wrote Philippians?
2. When was it written?
3. Where was it written?
4. To whom was it written?
5. Where in Scripture is it recorded that Paul founded and established the church at Philippi? What incident happened during this time?
6. Memorise verse 6.
7. What does verse 6 mean?
8. What is Paul's relationship with the Philippians like?
9. Read verses 9 to 11. Pray this prayer for yourself, then your family or friends.
10. Read verse 12. What has happened to Paul that he says 'really served to advance the gospel'?
11. Read verses 12 to 18. What is Paul's attitude towards:
    a) being imprisoned
    b) others preaching the gospel in order to stir up trouble for him?
    Write down what you can learn from this.
12. Paraphrase verse 20.
13. Meditate on verse 21.
14. What does this passage convey of Paul's relationship with Christ? Spend a few minutes asking God to give you a deeper relationship with Him.

Bible Study 2
Philippians 1:27—2:18

Read the passage at least three times.
1. Read verse 27. How can we 'conduct ourselves in a manner worthy of the gospel of Christ'?

2. Read verses 27 and 28. Paul speaks in these verses quite clearly about unity. Find another passage of Scripture where unity is taught as important.
3. Meditate on verse 29. Write down what God says to you.
4. What is your response to suffering? What should our response be? Look at James 1:2–4 and 1 Peter 4: 12–19.
5. Compile a list from chapter 2 as to what attributes a Christian should have.
6. Read verse 3. What is selfish ambition? And vain conceit? Spend a few minutes examining yourself before God. Repent of any selfish ambition or vain conceit in you now or in the past.
7. How easy/hard do you find verse 4?
8. Write down the qualities of Jesus according to verses 5 to 8.
9. Where in Scripture does it show Jesus as a servant?
10. Memorise verses 9 to 11.
11. Read verse 12. What does it mean to 'work out your salvation'?
12. Paraphrase verses 12 and 13.
13. Meditate on verse 14. Write down what God says to you. What is the main thing God has said to you through the study of this chapter?

Bible Study 3
Philippians 2:19—3:21

Read the passage at least three times.
1. Timothy was one of Paul's companions and fellow workers. They had a special relationship together. Find the story in Acts where Paul first met Timothy and took him with him on his journeys.

2. What do verses 20 to 22 portray of Timothy's character?
3. Read verse 25. Why was Epaphroditus with Paul? Also see chapter 4, verse 18.
4. Chapter 3, verse 1 exhorts us to 'rejoice in the Lord'. How do we practically do this?
5. Read verse 3. What does it mean to have 'no confidence in the flesh'?
6. Read verse 7. What kinds of things could you consider loss for the sake of Christ?
7. Paraphrase verses 10 and 11.
8. Meditate on verse 12. Write down what God says.
9. Choose a verse from this chapter and memorise it.
10. Read verse 13. What kinds of things in his past would Paul be choosing to forget? What can you learn from this?
11. What does verse 18 tell us of Paul's heart towards the unsaved?
12. Verse 19 speaks of people who have their minds on 'earthly things'. How do we practically keep our minds on heavenly things yet at the same time live here on earth?
13. Read verse 20. Do you 'eagerly await a Saviour from heaven'? Spend a few minutes praying about Jesus' return.
14. What are the main points of this chapter?

Bible Study 4
Philippians 4

Read the chapter at least three times.
1. What is the main point Paul is trying to convey through this chapter?

2. Memorise verse 4.
3. Meditate on verse 6. Write down what God says to you.
4. Write down any things that you are anxious about at this time. Spend time praying and presenting your requests to God.
5. If you do this, what does Paul say will happen in verse 7?
6. Paraphrase verses 6 and 7.
7. What can you learn from verse 8?
8. Look up 1 Timothy 6:6 as to how Paul values commitment. What does commitment mean to you? Are you content with your circumstances and place in life—or are you always striving for more?
9. What is the difference between earthly striving and striving for heavenly gain?
10. Meditate on verse 13. Write down what God gives to you.
11. What was the Philippians' attitude towards Paul and his companions who were working full-time for the Lord? See verses 10 to 19. What should our attitude be to missionaries or those working full-time for the Lord?
12. What is the main thing God has spoken to you about through this chapter?

Bible Study 5
2 Thessalonians 1

Read the chapter at least three times.
1. Who wrote 2 Thessalonians?
2. When was it written?
3. Where was it written?

4. To whom did he write?
5. Why was it written?
6. Read verse 3. What are the two things that are growing in the church in Thessalonica? Are these things growing in you?
7. Read verse 4. What were the two things that helped the church in Thessalonica to endure their trials and persecutions?
8. Spend time asking God to increase your faith and perseverance in the face of trials.
9. Verse 6 says, 'God is just: He will pay back trouble to those who trouble you'. Find another verse in the Bible to back this up.
10. Paraphrase verses 8 to 10.
11. Pick a verse from this chapter and memorise it.
12. What is the main thing God says to you through this chapter?

Bible Study 6
2 Thessalonians 2

Read the chapter at least three times.
1. What is Paul trying to convey through this chapter?
2. Why were the Thessalonians alarmed and upset?
3. Verse 4 tells us that the 'man of lawlessness' will set himself up against God. Look up Psalm 110:1. How will God deal with all who oppose Him?
4. Read verse 7. What does this verse mean?
5. Read verse 8. What does this verse say to you about God's power.
6. How can we tell the difference between God's miracles and Satan's counterfeit miracles? What must we do to keep from being deceived?

7. Verse 13 says we are 'chosen' by God. Spend a few minutes meditating on the fact that you are chosen. Write down your feelings.
8. Meditate on verse 14. Write down what God says to you.
9. Where else in the Bible does it say to 'stand firm'?
10. Memorise verses 16 and 17.
11. Encouragement is very important for us as Christians. When was the last time you encouraged someone else? Write down ways in which you could encourage your friends or family.
12. Ask God to encourage you and give you a greater desire to encourage others. Write down anything God says to you.

Bible Study 7
2 Thessalonians 3

Read the chapter at least three times.
1. What is Paul trying to communicate through this chapter?
2. How much emphasis and importance does Paul put on prayer and why?
3. Read verses 1 and 2. Paul exhorts us to pray for two things—what are they?
4. Spend time praying for these two things for yourself and your friends.
5. Meditate on verse 3. Write down what God says to you.
6. Verse 3 tells us the Lord is faithful. Write down many other qualities of our God.
7. What does Paul think of those who are idle?
8. Why is idleness wrong?

9. Examine yourself and see if there is any form of idleness in you. Spend time asking God if He sees any form of idleness in you. If so, then take a few minutes to pray and repent.
10. What verse(s) speak(s) to you the most and why?
11. Memorise that verse or verses.

REMEMBER

> *If you are fasting – it is very important to prepare yourself. See Chapters 2 and 3.*

Self Check List

1. Pride
2. Envy
3. Jealousy
4. Bitterness
5. Bad temper
6. Selfishness
7. Insensitivity
8. Unbelief
9. Ingratitude
10. Slander (i.e. speaking behind someone's back about their faults, etc.)
11. Lying (any kind of deception, i.e. hiding the full truth —perhaps only speaking half-truths)
12. Lack of love or respect for God
13. Wrong attitudes (particularly relating to prayer/Bible reading/church duties, etc.)
14. Lack of love for non-Christians
15. Worldly-mindedness (i.e. loving possessions and

money more than God—acting as though you have a 'right' to them)
16. Robbing God (e.g. money, time, etc.)
17. Greed
18. Hypocrisy
19. Lust of the flesh
20. Negative or critical attitudes
21. Hardness of heart

Mini Programme 13

Day One

15 minutes	Write down any specific aims you may have in spending this time with God and ask Him to begin to fulfil them over the next few days.
30 minutes	Read John 16:5–33. Write down what God says to you through these verses. Spend time praying thereafter.
15 minutes	Spend time praising God. Use some biblical ways of expressing your praise, i.e. singing, clapping, dancing, shouting, kneeling, raising hands, etc. Try expressing your praise to God in ways you haven't used before. It might be good to use a praise tape for this (see Chapter 7 and Appendix 2).
30 minutes	Go for a walk. Ask God to speak to you through nature. Write down what He says. Praise Him for His love for you.
30 minutes	Answer the following questions:

1. What is your deepest desire?
2. Do you feel secure in your friendship with God? If not, why not?
3. What kind of picture do you have of God?
4. What do you want God to do for you?
5. What do you want to do with your life? What are you aiming for?
6. What are you doing practically to outwork your answer to No. 5?

90 minutes	Bible Study 1.

30 minutes	Meditate on John 16:33. Write down what God says to you.

Day Two

30 minutes	Read Isaiah 62. Write down what God says to you through this chapter. Spend time in prayer thereafter.
30 minutes	Go for a walk. Ask God how He feels about you and for a picture of how much He loves you. Write down what God says.
45 minutes	Read Hebrews 12 twice. Write down what you get from this chapter then answer the following questions:

1. In verse 1, who are the 'cloud of witnesses?
2. In verse 2, how do we practically 'throw off everything that hinders and the sin that so easily entangles'?
3. Write down what things in your life would 'hinder' you or any sins that would easily 'entangle' you.
4. Ask God for His forgiveness and cleansing for the above and ask the Holy Spirit to fill you anew.
5. How do you react to discipline (verse 7)? And how should we react?
6. Verse 14 tells us to be 'holy'. Look up the word 'holy' in a dictionary. How do we become holy?

15 minutes	Go for a short walk. Meditate on James 1:22 while you walk. Write down what God says to you through your meditation.

90 minutes   Bible Study 2.

30 minutes   Make a list of all the good things God has done for you throughout your life and spend time praising Him for them. Use some biblical ways of expressing your praise, i.e. singing, clapping, dancing, shouting, kneeling, raising hands, etc. Try expressing your praise to God in ways you haven't used before. It might be good to use a praise tape for this (see Chapter 7 and Appendix 2).

Day Three

30 minutes   Read Psalm 145. Write down all God says to you through this Psalm. Spend time praising Him for all His faithfulness.

30 minutes   Answer the following questions:

1. Do you have any non-Christian friends? If not, why not and how could you develop friendships with others who are not Christians in order to help them?

2. Do you pray for any non-Christians regularly?

3. How often do you pray for the rulers of your nation?

4. Do you pray for God's influence to come in the media? in education? in politics?

5. Do you pray for the children of your land who are being abused, etc.? (You only need to pick up a newspaper to see many stories of hurt children.)

6. Spend five minutes praying about each subject above, i.e. the government, education, media, etc.

30 minutes   Read 1 Timothy 6:3–21. The downfall of many people can be the 'love of money'. How do you cope with money? Answer the following questions:

1. Do you feel that tithing is necessary?
2. Do you tithe your money faithfully each week/month?
3. Are you a generous giver?
4. Do you grudge spending money on yourself?
5. What would you do if you saw someone in need, but had already given your tithe for this month?
6. Have you ever had to 'live by faith'— in other words completely depend on God for finance? If so, what was your experience? If not, what would be your reaction if God asked you to do so?
7. Examine yourself—does everything in your life revolve around money?
8. What does Paul tell us in this chapter to pursue?
9. Is there anything wrong in being rich, according to this chapter?
10. If we are rich, how does Paul tell us to act?
11. What can you learn from this chapter, and the answers to the above questions, about yourself and money?
12. Spend a few minutes asking God if there is anything He wants to say to you

	about your finances. Write down anything He says and put it into practice as soon as you can.
30 minutes	Go for a walk. Pray for non-Christian family or friends as you walk.
90 minutes	Bible Study 3.
30 minutes	Pray with your leader/counsellor/pastor if appropriate or spend time praying about all God has said to you today.

Day Four

| 30 minutes | Read Isaiah 65:17–25. Write down what God says to you through these verses. |
| 30 minutes | Answer the following questions: |

1. Do you have a fear of the future? If so, which aspects of the future worry you and why?
2. Are you afraid of death?
3. Do you often think of Christ's return?
4. Which emotion do you portray when you think of Jesus coming back again?
5. Look up Philippians 1:21. In all honesty, could you say what Paul has said here? If not, write down your reasons why.

| 15 minutes | Go for a walk. Pray about Christ's return to earth as you walk. |
| 30 minutes | Read 1 Thessalonians 4:13–18 and 1 Thessalonians 5:1–11. Answer the following questions: |

1. 1 Thessalonians 4:18 and 5:1–11 say we should 'encourage each other'.

After reading these verses, do you feel encouraged and why?

2. Read chapter 5, verse 6. What can we do practically to outwork this verse?

3. Meditate on chapter 5, verse 10. What does God say to you through this verse?

4. Write down the main things God says to you through these verses.

90 minutes   Bible Study 4.

45 minutes   Spend some time praying about your answers to the questions in today's programme. If you need to repent of anything, then do so. If you need more of God's love, then ask God for it. Whatever you need to be more in love with Jesus and to welcome His return, then ask God for it in prayer. Then spend time worshipping God for who He is—for His plans for your life and for His plans for the world. Use some of the biblical ways to worship, i.e. singing, raising hands, speaking, kneeling, bowing, lying prostrate, etc. It might be good to use a worship tape (see Chapter 7 and Appendix 2).

Day Five

30 minutes   Read Psalm 24. Write down all that God says to you through the Psalm. Spend a few minutes praying about what God says.

30 minutes   Revival always begins in the church!

1. Spend time examining yourself and your life to see if there is anything God

183

would like to change.

2. Go through the self check list on pages 176 and 177 and see if any of these wrong attitudes are in you.

3. Spend time praying and repenting of anything God highlights.

4. Take a note of anything God tells you to do (e.g. apologise to someone; change attitude, etc.).

30 minutes   Go for a walk. Pray for revival for your nation as you walk. Ask God to give you a revival heart.

30 minutes   Ask God how He feels about the following subjects. Spend a few minutes on each. Write down what God says.

1. Your nation as a whole
2. The media
3. Crime and violence in your nation
4. The many injustices that happen
5. The poor and needy

Pray about the following subjects, spending a few minutes on each subject:

1. Violence in your nation
2. Abortions
3. Child abuse (physical and sexual)
4. Homelessness
5. The poor and needy

90 minutes   Bible Study 5.

30 minutes   Pray with your leader/counsellor/pastor—or spend time looking through all your notes and thanking God for all He's done in you during the last five days.

Appendix 1

RECOMMENDED BOOKS

This is not an extensive list. Choose a story book rather than a study book if possible.

Book Title	Author	Published by
No Compromise	Melody Green	Word Books
Another Way of Seeing	Marilyn Baker	Word Books
Building a People of Power	Ian Andrews	Word Books
God's Secret Angels	Dr Billy Graham	Hodder & Stoughton
God Can Do It for You	Ian Andrews	Word Books
Living on the Devil's Doorstep	Floyd McClung	Word Books
The Man in the Mirror	Patrick Morley	Word Books
China Cry	Nora Lam	Word Books
Seeking God	Joni Eareckson	Word Books
Good Morning Holy Spirit	Benny Hinn	Word Books
Twice Pardoned	Harold Morris	Word Books
How Will I Tell My Mother?	Jerry Arterburn	Word Books
Being Frank	Frank Gamble	Word Books
Appointment in Jerusalem	D. & L. Prince	Kingsway
Battle for Israel	L. Lambert	Kingsway
The Cross Behind Bars	J. Cooke	Kingsway
The Father Heart of God	Floyd McClung	Kingsway
History of Ishmael Part 1	Ishmael	Kingsway
I Dared to Call Him Father	B. Sheikh	Kingsway
Nine O'Clock in the Morning?	D. Bennett	Kingsway

Bible Study Books
How To Study Series

Enjoying God's Grace	Terry Virgo	Word Books
Facing Life's Problems	Frank Gamble	Word Books
Honouring Marriage	J. & L. Wilthew	Word Books
Receiving the Holy Spirit and His Gifts	Terry Virgo & Phil Rogers	Word Books
Prayer: Key to Revival	Paul Y. Cho	Word Books

Books on Fasting

God's Chosen Fast	A. Wallis	Kingsway
How to Fast Successfully	D. Prince	Word Books
Greater Health God's Way	Stormie Omartian	Word Books

Appendix 2

RECOMMENDED PRAISE TAPES

Heartbeat
Songs for a New Generation   Word UK
I Will Speak Out   Word UK
Celebrate   Word UK

Ian White
Psalms Volume 1   Little Misty Music
Psalms Volume 2   PO Box 8
Psalms Volume 3   Perth
Psalms Volume 4   PH2 7EX
Psalms Volume 5

Friends First
Here I Am   Word UK

Ric and Patty Ridings
Pray for the City   Word UK

Chris and Laura Christensen
Time to Fly   Word UK

Graham Kendrick
We Believe   Word UK
Amazing Love (Hosanna Series)   Word UK
Lamb of God (Hosanna Series)   Word UK

Chris Rolinson
Electric Praise   Word UK
Electric Praise Volume 2   Word UK

Noel Richards
By Your Side   Kingsway

Dave Bilborough
In the Name of the Lord   Kingsway
Sacrificial Love   Kingsway

Appendix 3

CARING ORGANISATIONS

Tear Fund
100 Church Road, Teddington, Middlesex, TW11 8QE
Tel: 081-977-9144

Care Trust
53 Romney Street, London SW1P 3RF
Tel: 071-233-0983

Shaftesbury Society
18–20 Kingston Road, London SW19 3RF
Tel: 081-542-5550

Jubilee Campaign
PO Box 80, Cobham, Surrey, KT11 2BQ
Tel: 081-892-3637

Caring Professions Concern
Church House, 34a Hilltop Road, Earley, Reading, Berks RG6 1DB
Tel: 0734-660515

Salvation Army
National Headquarters, 101 Queen Victoria Street, London, EC4P 4EP
Tel: 071-236-5222

Appendix 4

LETTERS

Here are some more letters from people who have completed some of my programmes.

Eileen from Swindon wrote to say:

Thank you for your extremely useful programmes. They gave me the opportunity to spend time honestly examining and assessing my personal walk with God and to practically implement biblical principles into my life.

Some questions ask you to empathise, either with a character from the Bible or in a hypothetical present-day situation, and explain how you would feel/react. From looking back at my answers, I can find the strengths and weaknesses to my reactions in those given situations and it highlights areas in my life that need change.

The way your programmes always included enough time for personal prayer to get right with God concerning the issue being studied was so beneficial.

By completing your programme I feel I have matured as a Christian because of recognising and actively dealing with various issues in my life.

One of the things I have learnt is the fundamental importance of actually giving time just to listen to God and it was during these times that I felt particularly close to Him. Thanks once again.

Shaz from Devon writes:

> *Just a note to say how much your pro-*
> *grammes helped me. I was able to focus on*
> *God and let Him deal with the issues I was*
> *praying about. Discipline has never been a*
> *strong area in my life and so your*
> *programmes were therefore very good for me.*

Jo from Portsmouth writes:

> *I found it so much easier to fast and pray*
> *using the programmes you prepared—moving*
> *though different forms of giving and receiving*
> *from God; meditation on scripture; prayer;*
> *answering questions and then taking a walk*
> *to let it all soak in; taught me to be more*
> *creative in prayer and more expressive.*
>
> *I believe that your programmes are*
> *inspired by the Holy Spirit and will be an*
> *encouragement and fresh challenge*
> *particularly to many people like me.*

Robbie from Maidenhead wrote also to say:

> *I want to say that I found your programmes to*
> *be very valuable. I found they helped me to*
> *seek God in a much more structured and*
> *useful way, as well as providing a more*
> *interesting study of the Bible.*

Some letters focused specifically on fasting. For example,
Danny from Bristol wrote to say:

> *Fasting is usually quite a difficult activity,*
> *especially when, like me, your attention span*
> *is quite short. Using your programmes I've*
> *found a focus in my prayer and meditation on*

189

God's Word. I enjoy the diversity of acti-
vities, like short walks where God speaks to
you through nature, etc. At the end of the day,
I have a written record of what God's said to
me, as well as a greater understanding of the
scriptures. So thank you again.

Sandy from Wales says:
I had never fasted for more than one day
before and going without food for two whole
days took a few prayers to settle my nerves!
In the morning of the first day I was
surprised to note that I was enjoying it.
Taking a few days out to read the Bible and
seek God's heart was really helpful.
I learnt a lot from your programmes, and
the Bible studies were relevant and thought-
provoking. I feel my relationship with my
Father really grew.

Pete from Belfast comments:
Having experienced the difficulties of fasting,
especially maintaining a focus during the
day, I found your programmes really helpful
in my prayer times and providing thoughts on
a particular aspect of God.
I was amazed how much I enjoyed fasting
and how fruitful my time with God was.

Phil from Bristol says:
I find fasting hard at the best of times, but I
found the structure in your programmes very
helpful in focusing my thoughts away from
food and on to God.
I also found it very helpful that in the
programme there was time given to meditate
and pray.

About the Author

Nancy Goudie has been involved in full-time Christian ministry for 12 years. She became a Christian when she was only six and for the first 22 years of her life attended a Brethren church in her home town of Ayr, Scotland. During her teens she became part of a well-established Christian band called Unity, where she was one of the vocalists. As well as singing she put her qualifications in speech (A.L.C.M.) to good use by being the narrator in the musicals that Unity produced.

Along with her husband she joined British Youth For Christ in 1980, where they directed the Creative Arts Department. Over the years she has sung with many different artists such as Sheila Walsh and Graham Kendrick. As founder and part of the band Heartbeat, she has not only sung and performed in all the UK's major venues, but has also had many opportunities to speak and lead seminars throughout Britain and abroad. She has appeared on television numerous times singing and speaking both in Europe and in the States.

Although she is used to ministering to large audiences, Nancy is very much a 'people person' and has been used by God to get alongside and help many who have needed God's love and healing. The Lord promised Nancy that He would give her 'spiritual children' who would need the comfort and care of a loving 'spiritual parent'. The Lord's promise has certainly been fulfilled as she has spent much of her time helping people of all ages to discover Jesus and the freedom and love that He can bring.

Nancy and her husband Ray, have one son, Daniel, and are currently the directors of the pioneering youth ministry, New Generation Ministries.

New Generation Ministries

New Generation Ministries is led by Ray and Nancy Goudie. In 1980 they were the leaders of the music ministry team of British Youth For Christ. During this time Ray and Nancy formed the band Heartbeat and left the salaried staff of BYFC to became a faith-based ministry involved in evangelism, training, worship, media and mission.

Since 1985 God has burned in their hearts a deep desire for revival and a strong conviction that a new outpouring of His Spirit was going to take place in the nations of this world. As their ministry continued to develop and in line with their growing vision to see a new generation reached for God, they changed their name in 1989 to NGM. With Heartbeat finishing in 1991 a new chapter had begun, with God promising even greater blessing as they continued to bring the good news to this needy and hurting generation. They are presently writing and recording a new youth musical/presentation and it is exciting to see the music from the NGM stable live on.

Part of their ministry is their recruiting, training and placing of young bands/teams to work alongside churches in evangelism and discipleship. Already they have placed bands in Swindon, Bristol, Southampton and in the needy city of Brussels.

The NGM bands, 65dBA, who are based in Britain, and Rhythmworks, who are based in Belgium, are already making a great impact throughout Europe. A cassette of the bands is available direct from NGM or through Word UK.

CAN YOU HELP?
The battle for our young people is raging. Please join with us and help to see God raise up this new generation for Him.

Ray and Nancy Goudie

THREE WAYS YOU CAN HELP

1. You can volunteer for one of the teams/bands and work on the frontline.
2. You can give money and support our work with young people in the UK and abroad.
3. You can pray for us. Thank you.

Please write for further information to:
NGM , PO Box 48, Malmesbury, Wiltshire , SN16 OHR